The Learning Curve: Towards a Better Education System

Steven Schwartz
Editor

Connor Court Publishing

The Learning Curve: Towards a Better Education System
Steven Schwartz (Editor)

Published in 2025 by Connor Court Publishing Pty Ltd

Copyright © The Centre for Independent Studies, 2025

All rights reserved. No part of this book may be reproduced or transmitted in any form or by any means, electronic or mechanical, including photo copying, recording or by any information storage and retrieval system, without prior permission in writing from the publisher.

Connor Court Publishing Pty Ltd
PO Box 7257
Redland Bay QLD 4165
sales@connorcourt.com
www.connorcourt.com

The Centre for Independent Studies
Level 1
131 Macquarie St
Sydney
NSW 2000

Printed in Australia

ISBN: 978-1-923568-12-9

Front Cover Design: Karla Pincott

50 years OF IMPACT

THE CENTRE FOR INDEPENDENT STUDIES

Contents

Prologue: Why This Book, and Why Now? — 1

Section 1: The Science of Learning and Effective Teaching: Why What Works Still Isn't Working — 3

1 What is the Science of Learning? *Trisha Jha* — 6

2 Aligning Education Policy with the Evidence on How Students Learn. *Trisha Jha* — 9

3 Curriculum Reform Must be Based on Evidence, not Fads. *Jennifer Buckingham* — 12

4 Scientific Evidence for Effective Teaching of Reading. *Jennifer Buckingham* — 14

5 Being Explicit in Class is the Best Way to Lift Results. *Trisha Jha* — 18

6 Dealing with Disruption and Disorder in the Classroom. *Glenn Fahey* — 21

7 Teachers are not Therapists. *Glenn Fahey* — 24

8 Teaching Behaviour. *Tim McDonald* — 28

9 How to Improve Learning Outcomes. *Glenn Fahey* — 33

10 Some Critical Thoughts About Critical and Creative Thinking. *John Sweller* — 36

11 Why Inquiry-Based Approaches Harm Students' Learning. *John Sweller* — 42

12 Reimagining Teacher Professionalism: Why Standards Must be Part of Initial Teacher Education Reform. *Rebecca Birch* — 46

Section 2: Equity, Performance, and Accountability in Schools: What Gets Measured — and What Must Be Done — 53

13 Why We Need to Track Intergenerational School Performance. *Matthew Taylor and Robert Breunig* — 55

14 Lifting NAPLAN Results. *Trisha Jha* — 58

15 Learning Lessons: The Future of Small Group Tutoring. *Trisha Jha* — 62

16 High-Quality Education Addresses Society's Inequities. *Glenn Fahey* — 66

Section 3: Maths Matters — Numeracy, Anxiety & Foundations   69

17 Setting the Foundation for Success in Mathematics. *David C. Geary*   71
18 Screening That Counts: Why Australia Needs Universal Early Numeracy Screening. *Kelly Norris*   76
19 How Maths Anxiety Could Be Holding You Back. *David C. Geary*   84
20 What Does and Doesn't Work for Maths Anxiety? *Glenn Fahey*   87
21 Programs to Help Kids Who Fall Behind in Maths Do More Than Add Up. *Kelly Norris*   90
22 Myths That Undermine Maths Teaching. *Sarah Powell, Elizabeth M. Hughes, and Corey Peltier*   93
23 Early Numeracy Screening Will Help Prevent Students from Falling Behind in Maths. *Kelly Norris and Glenn Fahey*   100
24 Do the Maths or We Will Never Be a STEM Superpower. *Glenn Fahey*   103
25 Mathematics Requires Explicit Instruction. *Glenn Fahey*   106

Section 4: History, Civics, and Citizenship   109

26 Teaching National Shame. *Joanna Williams*   111
27 Will Generation Lockdown Write Good History? *Fiona Mueller*   117
28 Missed Chance for Civics. *Fiona Mueller*   119
29 The Argument for Debate: How School Debating Can Improve Academic Outcomes and Foster a Stronger Democracy. *Deidre Clary and Fiona Mueller*   121
30 The Way Forward for the Australian Curriculum. *Fiona Mueller*   127

Section 5: Higher Education — Universities, Students, and Standards   129

31 Why Stop at Ending HECS-HELP for Failing Students? *Steven Schwartz*   132
32 Make Universities Pay for Picking Poorly Prepared Students. *Steven Schwartz*   134
33 ATAR's Rising Relevance: Admission Standards and Completion Rates. *Rob Joseph*   137
34 Job-Ready Graduates 2.0. *Andrew Norton*   145
35 Freedom, Not More Red Tape, Will Save Universities. *Steven Schwartz*   149
36 Five Ways Universities Can Advance Free Expression. *Steven Schwartz*   152
37 Campuses Should Not Be Safe Spaces to Breed Intolerance. *Steven Schwartz*   155
38 Degree Inflation. *Steven Schwartz*   159
39 Déjà Vu in Australian Higher Education. *Steven Schwartz*   163
40 A Shorter Path to Teaching. *Rob Joseph*   166
41 Eliminating the F Word – Failure. Steven Schwartz   172

Section 6: Funding Reform and the Politics of Money 177

42 Education Policy Must Mature Beyond Calls for More Money. *Glenn Fahey* 179

43 How Not to Waste Gonski School Funding. *Trisha Ja* 182

44 Dollars And Sense: Time For Smart Reform of Australia's School Funding. *Glenn Fahey* 185

Epilogue: Reform That Works 191

Contributors 193

Acknowledgments 200

Prologue
Why This Book, and Why Now?

Steven Schwartz

Education is one of the few subjects that everyone — regardless of age, location, or political affiliation — claims to care about. Ask any politician to name their top priorities, and "education" will certainly be mentioned. Ask any parent, and they will rank education just after health. Even economists have learned to speak of 'human capital', viewing schooling as the vital elixir of national prosperity. And yet, despite the rhetoric, Australia's education system seems stuck. We are spending more, enrolling more, regulating more, and — ironically — learning less.

The Centre for Independent Studies has long been engaged in the education debate, and this anthology collects some of the best recent papers and opinion pieces. Jennifer Buckingham's pioneering work on phonics played a crucial role in launching the phonics check nationally. Her contributions, along with those of Trisha Jha, Glenn Fahey, and others, have addressed a variety of issues, from degree inflation and maths anxiety to behaviour management and the funding follies of the 'Gonski' era. In more than forty published essays, op-eds, and reports, the contributors gathered here have explored different aspects of a single question: why, when we have so much knowledge about how people learn, do our policies and practices frequently ignore it? This book aims to bring clarity to the answers.

Grouped into themes — teaching and learning, equity and performance, mathematics, civics, higher education, and funding — the essays in this book clarify that we are not suffering from ignorance, but from a failure of translation. We have the research. We even have the money. What we lack is the will to link evidence with action, and the institutional flexibility to acknowledge that some cherished ideas simply don't work.

This book isn't a rant against teachers, schools, or universities. Most are doing their best in tough conditions. It also isn't an exercise in nostalgia. No one's suggesting we bring back ink wells and Latin declensions. Instead, this is a call for seriousness. For too long, education reform has swung between magic thinking and bureaucratic tinkering. We've promoted equity without fairness, innovation without a scientific basis, and a curriculum driven by politics. In short, we've forgotten that the purpose of education is to educate.

This book aims to remind us of the progress we've made and the ground still to cover. Some arguments will be familiar, especially to those who've followed the Centre for Independent Studies over the years. Others may challenge assumptions or provoke disagreement. That, too, is part of the point. A healthy education system should not fear dissent but welcome it, just as it should foster open debate and question received wisdom.

So, why should anyone read this book? Because education is not just about schools and universities, education is a mirror. It reflects what we believe about ourselves, our society, and the future. If we get education right, everything in society becomes easier. If we get it wrong, no amount of remedial policy will undo the damage. This book does not claim to have all the answers. But it does offer a guide to asking the right questions, grounded in research, experience, and a firm belief that we can — and must — do better.

SECTION 1

The Science of Learning and Effective Teaching: Why What Works Still Isn't Working

It is one of the great ironies of modern education that we know more than ever about how children learn, yet research evidence too often fails to penetrate practice or policy. Over the past two decades, research in cognitive science has built a clear, consistent body of evidence about how students best acquire, retain, and apply knowledge. At the heart of this growing field — sometimes called 'the science of learning' — is the idea that explicit instruction, rather than discovery learning, best serves students, particularly novices.

Teachers who explain, model, guide practice, check for understanding, and revisit material systematically are not stifling creativity; they are laying the groundwork for it. In *What is the Science of Learning?* Trisha Jha debunks long-standing educational shibboleths and argues for a return to structured, knowledge-rich instruction. Her point is further elaborated in *Being Explicit in Class is the Best Way to Lift Results*, where she also describes how education policy is finally moving in that direction, even as implementation lags. In *Aligning Education Policy with the Evidence on How Students Learn*, Jha describes how the science of learning can be integrated into practical policies.

Two contributions by Jennifer Buckingham reinforce the need to underpin curriculum reform with evidence and to avoid the fads that sound impressive but have no research to back them up. In *Curriculum Reform Must be*

Based on Evidence, not Fads, she takes aim at 'learning progressions', and in her seminal report on the *Scientific Evidence for Effective Teaching of Reading,* she shows how explicit teaching supported by the science of reading can revolutionise reading instruction.

Of course, effective teaching is not just a matter of method — it requires a classroom environment conducive to learning. Glenn Fahey, in *Dealing with Disruption and Disorder in the Classroom* and *Teachers Are Not Therapists,* exposes how student disruption and fuzzy notions of wellbeing have overwhelmed many teachers. His critique is not a call for nostalgia, but a plea for clear expectations, consistent routines, and practical support. Tim McDonald reinforces this in *Teaching Behaviour,* arguing that proper behaviour should be taught explicitly and systematically, just like reading or arithmetic.

One of the more quietly radical pieces in this section is John Sweller's *Some Critical Thoughts about Critical and Creative Thinking.* Drawing on decades of work in cognitive load theory, Sweller argues that many cherished educational goals — creativity, critical thinking, even innovation — are impossible to teach in a generalised form. These capacities emerge from deep domain-specific knowledge. We don't become more critical or more creative by trying to do so directly, but by knowing more about an area and knowing it well. That, in turn, depends on what is taught and how it is taught.

Sweller points out the negative implications of putting the horse before the cart in *Why Inquiry-Based Approaches Harm Students' Learning.* He shows that we cannot expect to teach pupils generic problem-solving skills without first building a solid foundation of basic knowledge and skills.

The final article in this section is Rebecca Birch's *Reimagining Teacher Professionalism,* which turns the spotlight on the Australian Professional Standards for Teachers. Birch argues that these Standards, which guide accreditation and initial teacher education, are misaligned with the evidence-based principles championed throughout this section. While other essays in this volume emphasise classroom practice, Birch addresses the upstream issue of how teachers are trained and assessed in the first place. Drawing on the *Strong Beginnings* report and international models such as England's Early Career Framework, she makes the case for reforming the Professional Standards to reflect what we now know from cognitive science and high-performing systems: that good teaching can be defined, practised, and taught. In that sense, Birch's contribution completes the circle, linking the science of learning not only to what happens in the classroom but to how we prepare and develop the professionals who stand at the front of it.

Together, these pieces form a compelling argument — good teaching is neither mysterious nor ideological. It is knowable, teachable, and scalable. What remains is the institutional and political will to act on what we already know.

1

What is the Science of Learning?

Trisha Jha

This paper explores how cognitive science insights can inform effective instructional practices in Australian education. It critically examines traditional progressive educational philosophies that emphasise minimal guidance and experiential learning, contrasting them with evidence-based approaches grounded in cognitive psychology and neuroscience. The goal is to bridge the gap between research and practice to improve student outcomes.

Understanding How Students Learn

Cognitive science reveals that novices learn best when information is well-organised and built upon existing knowledge structures, or schemas, stored in long-term memory. Unlike experts, who possess broad and interconnected domain knowledge, students benefit from structured, explicit instruction that reduces cognitive load and supports meaningful learning. Research shows that engagement in activities like hands-on projects or digital tasks does not necessarily equate to deep learning if students are distracted from core content.

Critique of Minimal Guidance Approaches

Approaches such as problem-based learning, inquiry learning, and student-led discovery have been widely adopted but lack strong empirical support for novice learners. These methods often assume that students can independently construct knowledge effectively, which contradicts findings on how memory and cognition function. Studies indicate that unguided learning can overwhelm working memory and hinder long-term retention and understanding.

The Case for Explicit Instruction

Explicit teaching strategies—characterised by clear explanations, guided practice, and gradual release of responsibility—align closely with cognitive principles. Techniques such as the guidance fading effect, where teacher support decreases as student proficiency increases, enhance learning efficiency. This approach ensures that students receive structured support tailored to their current level of understanding, promoting deeper engagement and mastery of content.

Bridging Research and Practice

Translating cognitive science into classroom practice has been inconsistent across the education system. Initiatives like the Catalyst program in the Catholic Education Archdiocese of Canberra-Goulburn demonstrate how research from experts like E.D. Hirsch Jr., Barak Rosenshine, and John Sweller can be synthesised into practical teaching frameworks. Similarly, tools such as those offered online by Deans for Impact help educators apply cognitive principles directly to instruction.

Challenges in Curriculum and Pedagogy

Despite growing recognition of evidence-based practices, many curricula and pedagogical guidelines still reflect progressive ideals that prioritise individualised learning experiences over structured knowledge acquisition. Australia's educational goals emphasise personalisation and creativity, which, while valuable, must be balanced with a strong foundation in core knowledge and skills. Misconceptions such as "neuromyths" (e.g., learning styles, brain hemisphere dominance) further complicate efforts to implement scientifically sound practices.

Policy Implications

School systems can take actionable steps without navigating complex federal-state dynamics. Revising local syllabi to emphasise knowledge as the object of learning and ensuring content builds sequentially across year levels can strengthen curriculum coherence. Updating pedagogical advice to reflect cognitive science insights—such as prioritising explicit instruction and reducing reliance on unsupported theories—can also improve teaching effectiveness.

Conclusion

The integration of cognitive science into instructional design offers a promising pathway to enhancing student achievement. While progressive educational philosophies have shaped much of the current landscape, evidence increasingly supports structured, knowledge-rich, and explicitly taught curricula. By aligning policy, curriculum, and professional development with scientific findings, Australian education can move toward more equitable and effective outcomes for all students.

This is a summary of a Centre for Independent Studies research paper. The full paper can be found at https://www.cis.org.au/publication/what-is-the-science-of-learning/

2

Aligning Education Policy with the Evidence on How Students Learn

Trisha Jha

Teachers are constantly told to use evidence-based practices, and no teacher would purposely use ineffective methods. So why does Australia still have so many problems with students' education outcomes? It's a critical question. The answer: there's a lot of focus on 'evidence-based practice', but a lot less attention on what that really means. This makes it hard to guarantee best practice is common practice.

New Centre for Independent Studies research shows the way forward is to develop a better understanding of the 'science of learning' — the connection between: 1) insights from cognitive science and educational psychology about how students learn; and 2) the teaching practices supported (and not supported) by those insights.

If teachers and leaders can develop a strong understanding of the science of learning, it can provide a framework against which to assess practices and inform how we teach, rather than the current grab-bag of practices all bearing the label 'evidence-based'.

First, it's crucial to start with the science of how we learn. While humans have evolved for some learning to occur naturally (such as speaking one's native language), other learning needs to occur systematically and explicitly (such as learning to read, write, do mathematics and most of the other things taught in schools). This is referred to as 'biologically secondary knowledge'. Instead of being able to think critically and creatively or problem-solve as a transferable skill, these higher-order skills are the product of deep knowledge of different domains. We need knowledge to think with.

In addition, human memory plays a critical role in learning. Working memory — what is active in our mental workspace at any one time — is limited. The only way to make working memory more effective is to strengthen long-term memory. Therefore, cognitive load theory posits that instruction should be designed to account for these features.

All this tells us what makes learning happen. But what does it mean for teaching? The teaching approach best supported by the evidence is explicit instruction of a well-sequenced, knowledge-focused curriculum.

Explicit instruction is not just telling and/or showing students how to do something. It is a multi-step instructional sequence that begins with careful ordering of curriculum content to create a coherent sequence, exposure to new concepts in small steps taught through modelling and worked examples, consistent student practice and checking for understanding, and regular review and practice to ensure retention.

Because working memory is limited and knowledge retained in long-term memory is crucial to making working memory more effective, students should only be expected to engage in complex tasks once they have been shown how. Independent work, problem-solving, critical analysis and argument development become capstone teaching and learning activities — not the foundation. To find out how this worked in real classrooms and real schools, the CIS spoke to teachers and leaders who have moved their practice more towards explicit instruction.

A commitment to education equity first spurred these teachers to change their practice. Some students weren't making adequate progress, and the teachers also recognised that approaches focusing on student-led learning, inquiry and discovery favoured students who already benefitted from having significant of cultural and educational capital.

Leaders were also able to create motivation for change among their teachers by emphasising the education equity benefits of explicit teaching. These insights are key to making education work for all Australian students.

However, teachers also conveyed that, despite their enthusiasm, they faced barriers such as a lack of formal support or training from the education system. This often left them dependent on informal networks of like-minded teachers.

Additionally, within the teaching profession, myths and misconceptions persisted, particularly regarding the science of teaching and explicit instruction, in particular. To overcome these barriers, teachers desired a clearer articulation of the science of learning that busts myths, and support across the education system to deliver outcomes in the classroom.

At a time when teaching as a profession is under scrutiny and many are feeling the effects of burnout, those who participated in our research described the sense of professional fulfilment they experienced from re-orienting their practice towards the science of learning. One person remarked "[Using the science of learning] gives me a sense of my own intellectual purpose, I feel challenged by it. Otherwise, I don't know if I could stay in teaching, if I didn't feel like I had something that elevated me".

But a strong sense of purpose, motivation and enthusiasm isn't enough. The teachers and leaders we interviewed expressed a need for stronger guidance from policy leaders about the importance of the science of learning. They noted that while advice advocating explicit teaching was provided, it often conflicted with accompanying advice advocating student-led learning.

Therefore, implementing the science of learning at scale will require a combination of top-down (system-driven) reforms and bottom-up (school and teacher-led) actions. Policymaker-imposed barriers must be removed and targeted strategies — such as shining a spotlight on successful schools so others can learn from them — are needed. This approach supports schools in the areas where they need it to implement change while using the authority of the school system to guide schools on the change journey.

By creating a shared understanding of good teaching and what success looks like, systems and schools can put teachers on a path to deliver better outcomes for their students.

This opinion piece was originally published by *EducationHQ*.

3

Curriculum Reform Must be Based on Evidence, not Fads

Jennifer Buckingham

The importance of the curriculum — what students are expected to know and be able to do at each stage of school — by far outweighs jousting over funding, although it gets far less public attention.

Curriculum development is a balancing act and involves compromises and trade-offs. Children spend a limited number of hours in class each year, and there are many competing demands for this time: from foundational skills in literacy and numeracy, to general knowledge of the world and its history, health and physical activity, using technology, and now so-called general capabilities such as collaboration and creativity.

This balancing act is growing more fraught. There is strong advocacy to add to an already crowded curriculum in significant ways. Decisions have to be made about what to keep and what to jettison. These decisions must made with advice from subject matter experts, without recourse to superficial and dangerous propositions such as that from "21st-Century skills pioneer" Charles Fadel, who recently suggested trigonometry should be out and mindfulness should be in.

Care must be taken that the curriculum does not implicitly or explicitly prescribe teaching methods. In theory, the curriculum is agnostic about teaching. It specifies the content students should learn and the skills they should master but does not state how these things should be taught.

The Australian Curriculum says children should learn to calculate percentages by the end of Year 4 but has nothing to say about whether this should be learned sitting at a desk or playing in a sandpit. Schools make judgments about which teaching strategies are most likely to be effective.

However, in reality a curriculum can and often does encourage certain teaching practices. An example is the recommendation in the second 'Gonski' report to "strengthen the development of the general capabilities, and raise their status within curriculum delivery, by using learning progressions to support clear and structured approaches to their teaching, assessment, reporting and integration with learning areas".

Creating a set of learning progressions is not a straightforward exercise. It heightens the influence of curriculum on teaching methods, and drives a particular approach to assessment. The Gonski report proposes "developing the general capabilities into learning progressions that will provide a detailed picture of students' increasing proficiency".

There are two risks in this. One is that it will authorise and promulgate the misguided notion that general capabilities are independent of knowledge of facts and concepts – including the fallacy that "learning how to learn" is the ultimate goal of school education.

The other is that the proposed policies and practices overshoot the existing evidence base, and therefore risk wasting valuable time and resources – not least the time of teachers who generally already have a heavy administrative workload, and that of students whose education is at stake.

The general capabilities listed in the Australian Curriculum – digital capability, critical and creative thinking, personal and social capability, intercultural understanding, and ethical understanding – are inarguably valuable for the world of work and for life more broadly. The crucial questions are whether they are really generic skills that can be conceptually sequenced on developmental progressions, and if they can be taught and assessed separate from content knowledge. The evidence at the moment suggests the answer to both questions is no.

This opinion piece was originally published by *The Sydney Morning Herald*.

4

Scientific Evidence for Effective Teaching of Reading

Kerry Hempenstall and Jennifer Buckingham

One million Australian children are at risk of reading failure, with serious negative consequences for their quality of life and Australian society. This figure — based on the results of national and international literacy tests — is five times higher than the number of children reading scientists estimate to have serious learning difficulties.

As seen in the Figure below, children from disadvantaged backgrounds are five times more likely to have low literacy at school than their more advantaged peers, perpetuating a cycle of low educational attainment and poverty. One in three disadvantaged children arrives at school with very poor language skills, and the gap between the language-rich and the language-poor grows over time.

The Solution is Effective, Evidence-Based Instruction

Despite there being various causes of disadvantage, there is only one domain in which an education system can have a significant and sustained impact — by harnessing the power of improved instruction, especially in literacy in the early years of school.

Major reviews of research on reading not only agree on the key components of reading programs but also on the most effective way of teaching them. A review concluded, "That direct instruction in alphabetic coding facilitates early reading acquisition is one of the most well-established conclusions in all of behavioural science" (Stanovich 2000).

There are five essential and interdependent components of effective, evidence-based reading instruction — the five 'keys' to reading.

Proportion of children not reaching reading benchmarks in primary school

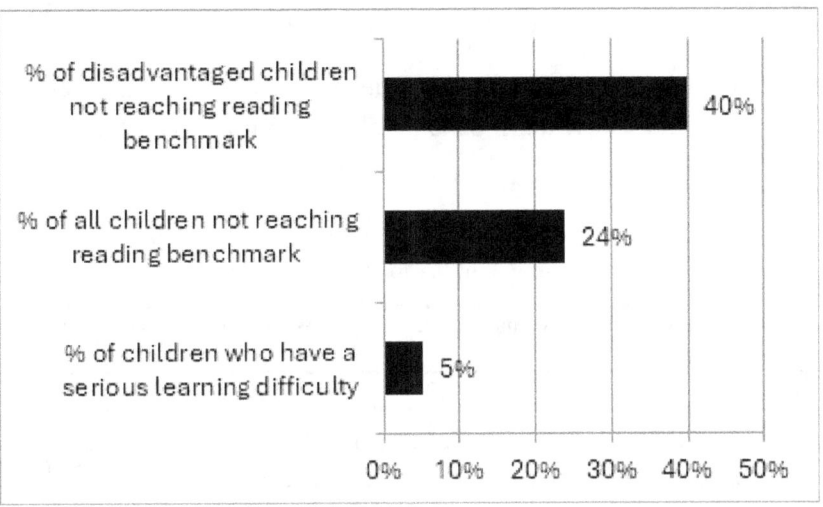

Source: Australian Council for Educational Research (2012); Kevin Wheldall (2011)

Five Keys to Reading

- Phonemic awareness: Knowledge of, and capacity to manipulate, the smallest distinct sounds (phonemes) in spoken words.

- Phonics: Learning and using the relationships between sounds and letter-symbols to sound out (decode) written words.

- Fluency: The ability to read accurately, quickly and expressively. Fluent readers can focus on reading for meaning.

- Vocabulary: The words children need to know to comprehend and communicate. Oral vocabulary is the words children recognise or use in listening and speaking. Reading vocabulary is the words children recognise or use in reading and writing.

- Comprehension: Extracting and constructing meaning from written text using knowledge of words, concepts, facts, and ideas.
-

Explicit Teaching is the Most Effective Method

There is also mounting evidence that explicit or direct instruction is the most effective teaching method, especially for the fundamental code-based components of reading — phonemic awareness and phonics — and especially for children at-risk of reading failure.

As seen in the Table below, research demonstrates that explicit teaching of the five keys to reading benefits all children and can significantly reduce literacy gaps.

Effect sizes from Hattie's meta-analysis (2009)
— Benchmark of 0.4 for 'real world' impact

Effective, evidence-based reading instruction	Constructivist/discovery approaches
Phonics 0.6	Whole language 0.06
Vocabulary programs 0.67	Exposure to reading 0.36
Comprehension programs 0.58	Student control over learning 0.04
Mastery learning 0.58	Mentoring 0.15
Worked examples 0.57	Inquiry-based teaching 0.31
Spaced practice 0.71	Problem-based learning 0.15
Feedback 0.73	
Questioning 0.46	
Direct instruction 0.59	

The impact of reducing the number of struggling students through more effective initial class teaching should not be underestimated. School resources and teacher time can be deployed more effectively, learning support can be targeted to children with serious learning problems, and benefits for students extend from improved educational achievement through to a lower likelihood of mental health and behavioural problems that frequently arise following reading difficulties.

The Research-to-Practice Gap Must be Bridged

Progress in knowledge of teaching and reading is dependent on evidence from studies that conform to the rigours of research in other disciplines where the human and economic costs of failure are high.

There is an extensive and rigorous body of evidence about how children learn to read and the most effective ways to teach them. While this research is slowly beginning to be acknowledged in government policy, unfortunately, it is not always reflected in teacher education or classroom practice.

This decade could be the beginning of one of the most exciting periods in education history, as the sleeping giant of educational knowledge — ignored for so long — begins to influence education systems around the world. If the evidence on teaching reading is adopted and implemented, there should be no more casualties in the 'reading wars'.

This is a summary of a research paper originally published by the Centre for Independent Studies. The full paper can be found on the Five from Five website at https://fivefromfive.com.au/wp-content/uploads/2022/07/Read-About-It.pdf. Five from Five is a community education initiative of MultiLit.

5

Being Explicit in Class is the Best Way to Lift Results

Trisha Jha

Welcomed by parents but dreaded by children, the 'Back to School' signs begin to emerge in shops of all kinds every January — a liturgical calendar alert in a secular age. The start of the year is also a time for resolutions: things to start, stop and improve. And some education-themed resolutions might help to stem the slide we've seen in Australian students' results over the past years.

While parents are not to blame for the problems in our education system, they can be part of the solution. For their children's sake, parents can — and should — become more discerning consumers of education, particularly if they are able to choose their child's school.

What do you know about what the leaders and teachers at your child's school think about how children learn best? You might think that the answer doesn't differ too much from one school or teacher to another, but that would be wrong. Studies show that high proportions of teachers believe in 'neuromyths' — false facts about how students learn, like the misconception that every child has their own 'learning style' that needs to be catered to in the classroom. Believing in false information can inform teaching practices in ways contrary to the evidence for how children learn and succeed: the 'science of learning'. This uses findings from cognitive science and educational psychology about human cognition (memory, encoding and retrieval) and applies them to teaching practice.

A key takeaway from this body of research is that explicit instruction (where teachers direct student learning through explanations, modelling and frequent questioning) is highly effective. This method contrasts with the 'student-led' inquiry approaches that are often encouraged on the basis they promote student engagement and therefore learning.

Far from being dull and mechanical, explicit instruction is highly interactive, where teachers respond to student learning needs and students are constantly engaging with their learning. Because these practices are informed by science, they can help improve student outcomes. It's no wonder, then, that explicit teaching has a new lease of life, with many states and territories implementing reforms that aim to move classroom practice in the right direction.

In New South Wales, updates to the syllabus mean more detail about what students should know, and how knowledge should build on itself, with the result a more ambitious plan for student learning. Victoria has announced a decisive shift towards evidence-based teaching of reading, and a new Teaching and Learning Model that uses the science of learning. Tasmania launched its Lifting Literacy plan, Queensland its Reading Commitment, and the ACT finalised its Literacy and Numeracy Inquiry report. But the difficulty for governments will be in implementation.

Addressing the classroom behaviour crisis is necessary to create fertile soil for well-intentioned reforms in teaching. OECD research shows Australian classrooms are among the most disruptive in the world, ranked 69th out of 76 countries and regions. The solution involves proactive training for teachers and clear systems of sanctions and consequences for students. Buying back classroom time for teachers to teach is not only key to improving learning, but might help with teacher retention too.

Parents have a role to play here too. A simple test of how well your child's school follows the evidence: how are the desks set up in classrooms? Are they in groups, in rows, or does the school leave this critical decision up to the teacher? Desks in groups are the classroom equivalent of the open-plan office: great for chatting, bad for those who want to get some work done.

Despite a popular belief that 'collaboration' (whatever that means) is vital to help student learning, it also means more opportunities for distraction, and has the potential to spiral into a vicious cycle of poor behaviour and poor learning. Seemingly small changes at the classroom level are vital if we want to see progress, but policymakers have a responsibility to get the settings right.

In line with the $16 billion federal funding deal currently on the table, states should agree to nationally consistent Year 1 checks in reading and number sense, targets improving NAPLAN performance and attendance, and use of evidence-based teaching methods that help prevent kids from falling behind, and providing the right kind of support if they do.

Governments are taking steps in the right direction, but 2025 must be the year of delivery. For the sake of our students, we can't wait another year.

This opinion piece was originally published by the *Daily Telegraph*.

6

Dealing with Disruption and Disorder in the Classroom

Glenn Fahey

The dismal state of student behaviour has long been the elephant in the classroom. To improve this, we must now put behaviour and classroom management at the centre of education reform.

Few statistics in Australia's education scorecard are more glaring than the poor performance in the OECD's 'disciplinary climate index' — an indicator of students' experience in class. Against this marker, the classrooms of Australian 15-year-olds are among the most disruptive and disorderly in the world, ranking at 69 out of 76 school systems. The same data shows that two in five students say their classmates don't listen to what their teacher says, and almost half say there is noise and disorder in most or all lessons. The toll on staff is also clear. Around one in four teachers find maintaining classroom discipline is difficult and that intimidation and bullying is common in around one in three schools.

Yet, like much in education, concern about behaviour has been all-too-often dismissed by many in the sector. Some simply believe that handwringing about behaviour is based on overly rigid expectations of uniformity, instead preferring to label any behaviour of students — however disruptive and unconstructive as it may be — as "authentic" displays of individuality. Others blame poor households, family structures, and technology. Yet others fear a behaviour emphasis implies a 'neo-conservative disciplinarian ploy to return corporal punishment' to schools.

But these objections are misplaced and fail to properly appreciate the role that facilitative class and school environments play in ensuring all students feel safe, secure, and ready to learn. In most cases, it is possible and appropriate to define objectively good and bad behaviour in school contexts. These common expectations help provide children with predictability and confidence in how they conduct themselves, what's acceptable and what isn't.

It's also unconvincing that out-of-school factors are solely responsible for worsening behaviour. Australia's classrooms have trended worse both against our own past results and those of other countries. It's hardly the case that better-performing countries don't experience similar out-of-school challenges to Australian students. And while the need to directly address behaviour is often downplayed by educational progressives, this misses the point that addressing behaviour in school is, at its core, a politically-progressive move to boost educational equity.

The greatest beneficiaries of clearer behavioural expectations — and classroom management to support it — are students who have been disengaged in schooling and those who don't have the benefit of consistently stable and supportive households. Moreover, orderly and calm classrooms benefit all students, no matter their ability or background.

To fix the crisis in school behaviour, policymakers must set a corrective path across three areas: promoting better practice, better information, and better supports. Better practice requires providing clear guidance to educators about the systematic use of evidence-based classroom management strategies. The best evidence suggests there's a 'big 5' for classroom management: maximising learning time; minimising off-task behaviour; establishing rules and routines; reinforcing positive behaviour; and addressing serious misbehaviour.

Federal education minister Jason Clare has engaged the Australian Education Research Organisation to develop resources to help teachers improve practice. However, this will only be effective if there is alignment with the — often contradictory — guidance given to schools from state bureaucrats. Better information requires opening the black box of classroom disruption and student behaviour.

While we report academic results in NAPLAN for each school, we don't transparently report on the experience inside classrooms. Recently-appointed NSW Behavioural Advisor, Donna Cross, has rightly made the case that decision-making on behaviour needs to be informed by data rather than anecdotes. In the UK, that has been addressed with a national behaviour survey of students and staff. And in the United States, several school systems publicly report on indicators of schools' learning climate.

Better support can ensure teachers have the tools they need to successfully deliver. As highlighted in recent CIS research, behaviour can — and should — be taught directly to students. A 'behaviour curriculum' clearly sets out year-level expectations for student behaviour; leaving little room for fuzzy interpretation. Teaching behaviour can be treated with the same emphasis as school subjects.

The training provided to teachers has often been insufficient to prepare them for managing challenging classrooms and students. A landmark teacher training review in July identified classroom management as one of four core areas in which all teachers will need to be trained in the future. However, the professional standards that teachers are rated against aren't currently explicit in how teachers should manage behaviour — leaving too much up to teachers to interpret for themselves. Instead, new teachers in England are provided with a clear framework that values managing behaviour as one of the key pillars of being successful.

Australia's education system has consistently been marked down when it comes to the behaviour of students and the capacity of teachers to manage classrooms. But policymakers can change course. In November, the Senate's Education and Employment Committee is due to hand down a report from its inquiry into the disruption and disorder of Australian classrooms. If done well, this could provide the much-needed blueprint to make behaviour the priority it must be.

This opinion piece was originally published by *The Australian Financial Review* as How to Turn Around Australian Kids' Appalling Classroom Behaviour.

7

Teachers are not Therapists

Glenn Fahey

New OECD data suggests Australia's long-declining performance in education has extended beyond academic results to students' lives.

Of course, we are now accustomed to disappointing international report cards when it comes to students' academic achievement levels. The OECD-run Programme for International Student Assessment has shown that the achievement of Australian 15-year-olds has suffered among the steepest and most consistent declines over the past two decades. However, these woes are now extending to other aspects of the school environment, with the latest report now pointing to troubling results in student behaviour and wellbeing in Australian schools.

The report not only shows that academic achievement has been generally disappointing, but that we also have relatively disruptive, unsafe, and unpleasant schools by world standards. On many yardsticks of students' wellbeing, Australia's school systems have been marked down — pointing to increasingly stressed, anxious, and vulnerable teens.

These twin crises in both behaviour and wellbeing issues have been mounting over recent years. Successive reports have shown the escalating scale of disruptive and disorderly classrooms in Australia. In the 2018 OECD Disciplinary Climate indicator, Australia ranked 69 out of 76 school systems; and in 2022, this was 33 out of 37 — deteriorating from a respectable ranking around the middle of the pack around a decade earlier.

There are some estimates that up to 20% of possible learning time is lost to avoidable disruption. The distractibility and lack of focus in class is, at least partly, coming from excessive use of digital devices in the classroom — of which Australian schools are among the world's most digitally-dependent.

Thankfully, on behaviour, policymakers have been responding appropriately — even if belatedly. The Senate's education committee handed down a landmark report late last year recommending that teaching degrees better prepare graduates with practical skills to manage classes and proposing an annual national survey to monitor what is happening inside classrooms.

Recently, education ministers agreed to work toward a framework for a national behaviour curriculum, which would result in clearer and more consistent expectations for how children should behave and what educators should prepare students to be able to do. In NSW, a chief behavioural advisor — modelled from a similar appointment in the UK — has been tasked with measuring, monitoring, and raising behaviour practice in classrooms across the state.

While we should expect these initiatives to bear fruit in coming years, there are broader concerns over physical and mental wellbeing that have been growing for some time now.

Australian students report being among the most bullied, around one in 10 don't feel physically safe at school, and one in five feel intimidated by their teachers. At the same time, increasing numbers of teachers also report being the subject of violence and abuse from troublesome students.

Mental health too has been a particular concern for teenage girls, and especially in the years since covid-19, the so-called 'shadow pandemic'. Overwhelmingly, Australia's teenage girls report struggling to cope with many school and life pressures; including regularly suffering anxiety and feeling nervous. Rising rates of so-called 'school refusal' — students who limit their engagement and attendance at school, largely because of mental health or related concerns — are symptoms of this problem. We must get back to basics in how we confront these additional crises of behaviour and wellbeing.

Unfortunately, although there is substantial evidence of the positive impact schools can make when it comes to both behaviour and wellbeing, misguided approaches from within the education establishment often make the problems worse. Much of the advice in the sector is overly academic or impractical, and emphasises reactivity rather than proactivity. Too often, the advice muddies rather than clarifies educators' roles on the issue.

Teachers end up being encouraged to be 'relationship managers' of students, dabbling as part-time therapists and psychoanalysts, often under the banner of so-called 'social and emotional learning'. Many of these efforts to promote 'social and emotional skills' are generally ineffective at best; and at worse, often backfire. Some programmes aimed at improving students' wellbeing can sadly make them worse.

There remains a critical need to ensure all students are welcomed into safe, supportive, and caring classrooms. But this should not extend to expecting teachers to tolerate bad behaviour in the name of 'inclusivity'. Effective behaviour management, unlike the punitive discipline of old, is an essential part of the teaching toolkit and crucial to improve student wellbeing as well. Although the major incidents of poor behaviour — like violence and exclusion —attract most attention, it's actually the everyday low-level disruption and distractibility that is most pervasive and telling of systemic issues.

Policymakers need to do better. While we have started down a better path on behaviour, there are important decisions ahead of the broader issue of wellbeing. Education ministers concluded late last year that there should be a wellbeing performance measure for school systems. But policymakers must resist the use of generic indicators — which often ask children about out-of-school issues like their general life satisfaction and circumstances — and instead should target in-school and manageable areas. This can help schools to take a measured and practical approach toward wellbeing matters and to focus on what teachers can do well: making constructive use of lesson time; having students enjoy opportunities for success; and promoting a generally supportive school community.

As a nation, we are rightly concerned about declining achievement outcomes and persistent inequities in the school system. But getting the classroom climate right in behaviour and wellbeing will go a long way to securing better learning outcomes. Australia can be both a clever country and a 'well' country when it comes to our students. But only if we ensure we take a practical and evidence-based approach to solving the challenges in our education system.

This opinion piece was originally published by *The Australian* as Let's Stop the 'Teachers as Therapists' Business and Get Back to Basics.

8

Teaching Behaviour:
How Classroom Conduct Can Unlock Better Learning

Tim McDonald

Australian classrooms can be loud, unruly places in which students find it difficult to learn. In a 2018 Programme for International Student Assessment (PISA) study of 15-year-olds, 43% of students surveyed said that they were in classrooms that were noisy and disruptive. This is well above the Organisation for Economic Co-operation and Development (OECD) average of 33%, and places Australia 69th of 76 countries on the 'disciplinary climate index', which means Australian schools are among the least orderly in the world. These statistics are telling, as orderly classrooms are a pre-condition for student learning.

In response to the increased awareness of the disruption in classrooms, the federal government, through its Senate Education and Employment Reference Committee, has launched an inquiry into "the issue of increasing disruption in Australian school classrooms". The inquiry also will examine what universities are doing to prepare teachers to deal with disruptive behaviour. Meanwhile, the government has set up the Teacher Education Expert Panel (the Panel) to give advice on key practices every teacher should learn in Initial Teacher Education (ITE) to prepare them for disruptive student behaviour.

The recommendations in the Panel's final report '*Strong Beginnings: Report of the Teacher Education Expert Panel*' are designed to strengthen ITE in Australia. The Panel identified the core content for ITE programmes that met the Graduate Teacher Standards and had the greatest impact on student learning. The other core content area was 'Classroom Management'. The report highlighted the need for graduates to know how to establish a classroom that enabled student learning. The Panel commented that classrooms that enabled student learning were characterised by clear expectations, supported by routines and rules to ensure students were safe and engaged in learning. In these engaged classrooms, the teacher models and gives feedback on expected behaviour rather than reacting to off-task behaviour.

The OECD Policy Perspectives Report (2023) notes that there is a "current need in Australian schools to strengthen learning environments to become fully conducive to learning". There is still work to do, as identified in the behaviour climate index rating with the added evidence that 37% of lower secondary Principals report that intimidation and bullying among students occurs at least weekly (TALIS, 2018). It is not just students that do not feel safe in classrooms or in school. In the same report, 28% of teachers identified maintaining classroom discipline as a stressor, and 13% reported being intimidated or verbally abused by students. The TALIS (2018) data is supported in the *'Perceptions of Teachers and Teaching'* study by Heffernan (2019), where 19% of teachers reported that they did not feel safe in classrooms or at school.

What is the Nature of Disruptive Behaviour in Australian Schools?

Research over the past 40 years is clear as to what distracts teachers from teaching. The behaviours that teachers find difficult to manage are often minor but high frequency and low-level. Low-level behaviours identified in the research involving Australian teachers were commonplace, such as talking out of turn, and avoiding work. The frequency and repetitive nature of these behaviours contributes to the disruption in the classroom for student learning and teacher instruction time and stress.

The Grattan report reflected this research on low-level behaviour: "the main problem is not aggressive or anti-social behaviour[,] as more prevalent and stressful for teachers are minor disruption[s]" (p.3). The report based these statements on the Pipeline Project (on which the author was a researcher), a significant longitudinal study conducted in Western Australia that resulted in a report titled *'Trajectories of Classroom Behaviour and Academic Progress: A Study of Engagement with Learning'*. The project sought to describe the kinds of student behaviour that were impeding students' academic progress. These were referred to as 'unproductive behaviours'.

The research paints a consistent picture of widespread low-level disengagement and disruption. It found that 40% of students displayed unproductive behaviours regularly in any given year. In this group of unproductive students, more than half were in a 'compliant disengaged' group, described by their teachers as uninterested in their schoolwork, unprepared for lessons, and quick to give up tasks they found difficult or boring. The most common unproductive behaviour identified by teachers was inattentiveness.

Disengaged students have an effect on academic achievement in classrooms across Australia. The Pipeline Project study tracked students over four years and found that unproductive students (40%) were, on average, one to two years behind peers in literacy and numeracy. Interestingly, the study highlighted that these quiet, yet disengaged, students did just as poorly as the students whom teachers identified as disruptive. John Hattie, referring to the Pipeline Project study, commented that 'these ambivalent [unproductive] students should be the focus of teachers attention — and are perhaps the easiest to win back'. Hattie's point highlights the reality that creating calm, orderly and inclusive classrooms in Australian schools is possible. There are evidence-based practices that teachers can use in their classrooms to effectively and efficiently create environments where all students learn.

Understanding the Role of Behaviour in Learning

Student behaviour significantly influences engagement and learning outcomes. Research indicates that low-level disruptions — such as talking over the teacher or not following instructions — are more detrimental to classroom dynamics than severe misconduct. These behaviours reduce instructional time and increase teacher stress, ultimately affecting student progress. Addressing these issues requires a proactive approach that treats behaviour as a skill to be taught rather than an inherent trait.

Critique of Current Approaches to Behaviour Management

Many schools rely on reactive strategies such as detentions or suspensions, which do little to teach appropriate behaviour. Some educators attribute misbehaviour to external factors like unmet needs or medical conditions, inadvertently removing student accountability. This perspective overlooks the potential for behaviour to be explicitly taught and reinforced through practice, feedback, and consistency—similar to academic skills.

The Case for Explicit Behaviour Instruction

Explicitly teaching behaviour involves breaking down expectations into clear, observable steps and providing structured opportunities for students to practise them. For example, routines such as lining up quietly, entering the classroom calmly, greeting the teacher, and sitting down attentively can be modelled, rehearsed, and corrected until mastered. This method aligns with cognitive science principles, particularly the idea that repeated practice and immediate feedback support habit formation and long-term retention.

Bridging Research and Practice

Schools that implement structured behaviour programs report improved classroom climates and fewer disruptions. One example is the use of scripted routines that guide students through daily transitions with precision. Programs like these ensure consistency across classrooms and year levels, reducing ambiguity and reinforcing expectations. Evidence from longitudinal studies supports this approach, showing that students who learn structured routines demonstrate greater self-regulation and academic engagement over time.

Challenges in Curriculum and Policy

Despite growing recognition of the benefits of explicit behaviour instruction, many curricula and policy frameworks do not prioritise it. Australia's national curriculum highlights capabilities such as literacy, numeracy, and critical thinking but does not formally include behaviour as a general capability. While appropriate conduct is implicitly valued, making it an explicit focus would help schools embed it systematically across all learning areas and developmental stages.

Policy Implications

To improve student behaviour at scale, policymakers should consider the following actions:

- Integrate behaviour as an explicit general capability within the national curriculum.
- Provide professional development for teachers on structured behaviour instruction and classroom routines.
- Encourage the adoption of evidence-based behaviour programs that align with cognitive science principles.
- Support schools in developing consistent expectations and practices across classrooms and staff.
- Monitor and evaluate the impact of behaviour initiatives using data on student engagement and academic progress.

These steps would help create school environments where positive behaviour is taught, practised, and reinforced, leading to improved learning outcomes for all students.

Conclusion

Student behaviour plays a crucial role in shaping effective learning environments. While current approaches often focus on punishment rather than prevention, research suggests that treating behaviour as a teachable skill leads to better outcomes. By adopting structured, explicit instruction in expected behaviours and embedding this approach within policy and curriculum, Australian schools can foster greater student responsibility, reduce disruptions, and enhance academic achievement.

> This is a summary of a Centre for Independent Studies research paper. The full paper can be found at https://www.cis.org.au/publication/teaching-behaviour-how-classroom-conduct-can-unlock-better-learning/

9

How to Improve Learning Outcomes

Glenn Fahey

The latest National Assessment Program – Literacy and Numeracy (NAPLAN) data set highlights the urgent need for the education system to set ambitious improvement targets to improve student outcomes. This year's NAPLAN results, released yesterday, indicate that student achievement levels are stable, but there is no clear evidence of improvement. This aligns with other indications of a stagnation, but not a reversal, in the trend of poor or declining education outcomes.

Over the past two decades, Australian student performance in the OECD's Programme for International Student Assessment (PISA) has shown some of the steepest and most consistent declines globally. The most recent PISA results, published late last year, showed little change. Similarly, NAPLAN scores have generally remained flat for over 15 years.

However, stagnant outcomes are not a sign of success in the education system. Beyond the lack of overall improvement, there is little evidence of reduced achievement gaps for disadvantaged students, or progress in helping those who fall behind to catch up. This is a disappointing legacy, but not surprising, given the unfortunate reality that too many in the sector have not prioritised education outcomes.

First, the focus for many has primarily been on the level and distribution of resources going into the system. The fallacy that increased funding alone would lead to improved achievement has always been misleading and cynical. More than a decade of Gonski funding, aimed at improving achievement and reducing gaps, has had minimal impact on outcomes.

Yet, spats over resources continue to dominate policy discussion. Education ministers are currently haggling over the funding split between Canberra and the states, despite substantial additional federal funding already being offered — and Australia's school funding increases being among the highest in the developed world for most of the past two decades

Second, education ministers and unions have preferred to undermine or abandon NAPLAN rather focus on improving success. Some have attempted to review NAPLAN out of existence. But it has withstood multiple independent reviews — each confirming its value as a crucial assessment of foundational literacy and numeracy.

Many school systems envy the nationally-consistent and easily-interpretable benchmark that NAPLAN provides. Despite its imperfections, NAPLAN become a better and more useful instrument for schools in recent years. Yet, unions have consistently opposed standardised testing in general and NAPLAN (including the MySchool website that publicly reports schools' NAPLAN results) in particular. This unproductive and adversarial approach — such as instructing union members to boycott the test — seems a shift away from supporting the sector, opting instead to obscure poor outcomes rather than address them.

Improving learning outcomes will be impossible as long as NAPLAN — the most reliable and widely available indicator — is not taken seriously. Therefore, policymakers must make enhancing education outcomes an explicit priority. Any school system committed to improvement starts by setting clear targets, and high-performing systems achieve success by actively managing outcomes rather than leaving them to chance. System targets for NAPLAN should be ambitious and concentrate on benchmarking improvements in how systems ensure students catch up, keep up, and move up in NAPLAN proficiency levels.

To its credit, the federal government has set modest improvement targets in NAPLAN in its new funding agreements with the states, which will be negotiated and finalised in the coming months. This follows two reviews over the past few years — one from the Productivity Commission and another from an expert panel —that outlined potential outcome measures for setting system targets.

However, state education systems don't have a strong track record in effectively measuring outcomes. Most rely on vague and woolly goals that often lack relevance to student achievement. In others, outcomes measurement has actually regressed. In NSW, the government recently ditched — as a "workload reduction" measure — the School Success Model that provided public schools with general targets, support to reach them, and state-wide achievement goals.

NAPLAN is one of the most valuable assets of Australia's education system. Policymakers must show they too value it by using it as an evaluation benchmark. Education improvements can only begin once ambitious and transparent targets are set.

This opinion piece was originally published by *The Australian.*

10

Some Critical Thoughts about Critical and Creative Thinking

John Sweller

Developing creative and critical thinking is a major priority of educators and policymakers. This is promoted because of popular views that students today require more creativity and critical thinking than past generations.

It is now common to find creativity and critical thinking featured in curriculum documents, teaching practice guides, and in student assessments. This is rarely, if ever, accompanied by an understanding of how students learn or evidence to support teaching or assessment approaches. This paper provides an overview of human cognitive architecture as relevant to how students learn and demonstrate such thinking. In doing so, it highlights that general 'creativity and critical thinking' is not something that can be taught. That's because we have evolved to do this innately without instruction. What does require teaching is the relevant knowledge base to allow students to properly apply these skills.

Overview

Creative thinking refers to producing ideas that are both novel and useful, while critical thinking involves evaluating information in ways that allow for revision of beliefs. Although frequently cited in education policy, these concepts are often defined in abstract terms, with little reference to practical strategies or examples.

In today's information-rich environment — rife with misinformation —

critical thinking is deemed increasingly essential. Creativity is similarly championed, particularly in political efforts to drive innovation, such as Australia's Innovation Agenda, despite the country's already high ranking in global creativity indices.

The push for these skills is also driven by economic considerations. Employers reportedly value critical and creative thinking more than ever, linking them to higher early-career earnings and influencing recruitment decisions through standardised tests. In response, schools are increasingly expected to teach and assess these skills, with critical and creative thinking now embedded in most curricula and even international assessments like PISA.

However, efforts to promote these skills often neglect insights from human cognitive architecture — our evolved system for processing information. Without understanding how people actually learn and think, attempts to teach thinking skills may fail or backfire. Instead of teaching strategies directly, students are frequently asked to solve novel problems in the hope this will build thinking ability, despite evidence that worked examples are a more effective approach. The lack of proven success in teaching general thinking skills reflects this misalignment. Since thinking is a cognitive activity, any instructional approach must align with our cognitive architecture — a point further explored in the next section.

Natural Information Processing Systems

To understand how humans think, it is useful to consider how information is processed in nature more broadly. Evolution by natural selection represents a highly creative natural information processing system. This system has generated the immense variety of life on Earth and can be analysed to understand the underlying mechanisms of creativity. These mechanisms may serve as useful analogies for human cognitive processes.

Evolution by Natural Selection

Evolution is not only a biological theory but also an example of a powerful, decentralised information-processing system. Its creative success can be explained through five principles:

1. **Random mutation** introduces novel genetic variations. Though most are maladaptive, some enhance survival and are preserved.
2. **Reproduction** passes on adaptive traits. Asexual reproduction replicates beneficial mutations exactly, while sexual reproduction combines genes, amplifying evolutionary success.
3. **Environmental influence** through the epigenetic system determines the timing and location of mutations. For example, snakes may mutate toxin-related genes more frequently in response to resistant prey.
4. **Genome construction** stores adaptive mutations across generations, acting as a long-term information repository.
5. **Phenotype regulation** relies on the environment to switch genes on or off, resulting in different cell types like liver and skin cells, despite identical genetic material.

Together, these processes form a natural, decentralised system that achieves creative outcomes without a controlling executive — unlike a computer. This same architecture underpins human cognition, allowing for creativity without requiring a central 'programme'. Understanding these parallels can enhance our grasp of how humans learn, think, and innovate.

Human Cognitive Architecture

Humans have evolved with two cognitive systems: one for biologically primary knowledge and another for biologically secondary knowledge. Biologically primary knowledge, such as speaking a native language or basic social interactions, is acquired effortlessly because it is essential for survival. In contrast, biologically secondary knowledge, like reading or algebra, is culturally important but not naturally acquired; it requires explicit teaching.

The five natural information processing principles apply only to biologically secondary knowledge, as each principle itself is a biologically primary skill. These principles function without a central executive, similar to evolution by natural selection. While biologically primary skills are generic (e.g., problem-solving), biologically secondary knowledge is typically domain-specific and must be taught to be acquired.

How We Acquire Novel Information

Novel, biologically secondary knowledge can be acquired either through problem-solving (analogous to random mutation in evolution) or from others (analogous to reproduction). Random generate-and-test is fundamental to solving novel problems when prior knowledge is insufficient. While this method underpins creativity, borrowing information from others—a biologically primary skill—is far more efficient.

Humans' unique ability to learn from others means students should be presented with information rather than left to discover it independently. While random generate-and-test is necessary for initial knowledge creation, education should prioritise transmitting existing knowledge efficiently.

How We Process and Store Novel Information

Once acquired, novel information is processed in working memory, which has strict limitations: it can handle only 3-4 novel elements at a time and retains them for about 20 seconds without repetition. Processed information is then stored in long-term memory, which has no known capacity limits and holds complex, organised knowledge essential for understanding even simple statements.

How Information Held in Long-Term Memory Facilitates Creative and Critical Thinking

Information from long-term memory can be transferred back to working memory to guide actions. Unlike its limitations with novel information, working memory has no constraints when processing familiar knowledge. Long-term memory shapes cognition and creativity, as all learned information—from facts to intricate concepts—resides there.

Implications for Educational Theory and Practice

Critical and creative thinking are often discussed without reference to human cognitive architecture. Effective teaching must account for working memory limitations, the role of long-term memory, and our evolved ability to learn from others. Current educational approaches often overlook these factors, leading to ineffective strategies.

Facilitating Critical and Creative Thinking

While educators emphasise developing critical and creative thinking, methods like self-discovery lack empirical support. Cognitive biases training and generic thinking strategies often fail because they neglect the importance of domain-specific knowledge. Instead, fostering critical thinking requires building a robust knowledge base in a given domain, as cognitive load theory suggests.

Measuring Critical and Creative Thinking

Assessments claiming to measure general critical thinking skills ignore cognitive architecture. Creativity tests inadvertently measure biologically primary problem-solving combined with domain knowledge, not teachable strategies. Without knowing a student's knowledge base, determining true creativity is impossible.

The Case for Optimism

Progress has been made in recognising that critical thinking is domain-specific, not general. However, some curricula still erroneously treat it as a transferable skill. Creativity is biologically primary, meaning students already possess it; teaching should focus on expanding domain knowledge to enhance its application.

Conclusions

Critical and creative thinking are biologically primary skills, not teachable generic strategies. Differences in students' abilities stem from variations in domain-specific knowledge, not from learned thinking techniques. Until evidence supports alternative creativity mechanisms, advocating for general critical thinking in curricula is unfounded. While future discoveries may change this, current educational practices should prioritise knowledge acquisition over unproven thinking skills training.

This paper challenges educators to identify any teachable generic thinking strategies with empirical backing. Without such evidence, efforts to teach critical and creative thinking as general skills remain unjustified. Instead, fostering deep domain knowledge is the most effective way to enhance these innate cognitive abilities.

This is a summary of a Centre for Independent Studies research paper. The full paper can be found at https://www.cis.org.au/publication/some-critical-thoughts-about-critical-and-creative-thinking/

11

Why Inquiry-Based Approaches Harm Students' Learning

John Sweller

The concept of inquiry learning, introduced 60 years ago, has evolved into terms like problem-based learning and constructivist learning, with inquiry learning being the most prevalent today. Initially grounded in the cognitive psychology of its time, it became widely adopted within two to three decades, particularly in Anglosphere countries, with minimal opposition until recently. Proponents argue that inquiry learning enhances general problem-solving skills and creativity, given humans' natural problem-solving abilities. It is posited to improve students' capacity to address novel problems creatively, benefiting society broadly. Additionally, inquiry learning is believed to facilitate deeper understanding of disciplinary concepts compared to rote memorisation, mirroring how researchers and individuals learn outside formal education. This approach is considered more engaging than traditional classroom methods, promising to make school learning as effective as real-world learning. However, as knowledge of human cognitive architecture has progressed, it increasingly challenges inquiry learning's efficacy. Data from randomised controlled trials and correlational studies further undermine its effectiveness, necessitating a re-evaluation of its role in education.

Human Cognitive Architecture

Human cognitive architecture, informed by evolutionary psychology, distinguishes between biologically primary and secondary knowledge, significantly impacting instructional design.

Evolutionary Psychology and Categories of Knowledge

Biologically primary knowledge, such as learning to speak a native language or general problem-solving, is acquired unconsciously and effortlessly due to evolutionary adaptations. These generic-cognitive skills, like means-ends strategies, are modular and unteachable, as they are inherently acquired without formal instruction. Conversely, biologically secondary knowledge, including reading, writing, and subject-specific skills like algebraic manipulation, is culturally significant but not evolutionarily ingrained. Schools exist to teach these domain-specific skills, which require conscious effort and often explicit instruction. The assumption that inquiry learning, effective for biologically primary skills in real-world contexts, should apply to secondary knowledge in schools overlooks this distinction. Inquiry learning may not enhance general problem-solving, a primary skill already acquired, nor is it necessarily the optimal method for acquiring secondary knowledge, an empirical question requiring further scrutiny.

Cognitive Architecture Associated with Biologically Secondary Information

The cognitive architecture for biologically secondary information involves five principles governing acquisition, processing, storage, and application. First, novel information can be generated through problem-solving via a random generate-and-test method, a slow and inefficient process reliant on biologically primary skills. Second, borrowing information from others—through listening, reading, or imitation—is far more efficient, leveraging humans' unique ability to share knowledge. Third, novel information is processed by a working memory with severe capacity (holding about seven items, processing three to four) and duration (lasting seconds without rehearsal) limitations. Fourth, processed information transfers to long-term memory, which has no known capacity or duration limits, storing complex, interconnected knowledge critical to expertise. Fifth, environmental cues trigger the transfer of stored information back to working memory, which has no capacity limits when handling familiar information, enabling action. The worked example effect, where students studying solutions outperform those solving problems, demonstrates explicit instruction's superiority, as it reduces working memory load compared to inquiry learning's demands.

Cognitive Load Theory

Cognitive load theory, grounded in the described cognitive architecture, generates instructional strategies through randomised controlled trials, comparing new methods to standard practices. The worked example effect exemplifies this, showing that studying detailed solutions reduces working memory load compared to problem-solving, which overwhelms novices with tasks like tracking problem states and goals. For instance, solving an equation like $((a+b)/c=d)$ for (a) burdens working memory, whereas studying a worked example streamlines learning by presenting steps clearly. This effect is consistent across disciplines, including mathematics, science, and literature. The expertise reversal effect further nuances this, indicating that as learners gain expertise, the advantage of worked examples diminishes, and problem-solving becomes more effective for practice. However, for introducing new material, explicit instruction remains superior. Correlational studies reinforce this, showing a negative relationship between inquiry learning emphasis and test scores, aligning with the theory's predictions.

Conclusions

Inquiry learning's prominence in curricula lacks theoretical and empirical support. Curriculum documents rarely acknowledge its cognitive implications, assuming learners' cognitive architecture does not interact with instructional methods. Inquiry learning neither enhances inquiry skills, which are biologically primary, nor effectively teaches secondary knowledge, as evidenced by the worked example effect. Randomised controlled trials consistently favour explicit instruction, particularly for novices, while the expertise reversal effect highlights problem-solving's role only for advanced learners. Correlational data from international tests, such as PISA, reveal that increased inquiry learning correlates with declining performance, explaining Australia's falling rankings. The absence of specific inquiry strategies in curricula further undermines its utility. A shift towards explicit instruction, supported by cognitive load theory, is warranted to reverse declining educational outcomes and align teaching with human cognitive architecture.

This is a summary of a Centre for Independent Studies research paper. The full paper can be found at https://www.cis.org.au/publication/why-inquiry-based-approaches-harm-students-learning/

12

Reimagining Teacher Professionalism. Why Standards Must be Part of Initial Teacher Education Reform

Rebecca Birch

Abstract

The Australian Professional Standards for Teachers, established in 2013, fail to clearly define what teachers should know and do, remaining neutral on effective teaching practices, thus requiring urgent reform. I advocate for aligning these Standards with the *Strong Beginnings* report's recommendations, which mandate four core content areas in initial teacher education (ITE): the brain and learning, effective pedagogical practices, classroom management, and responsive teaching. While *Strong Beginnings* draws on robust cognitive science showing similar human learning processes, the Standards overemphasise differentiation, implying diverse learning needs. As foundational to ITE and teacher accreditation, the Standards are critical to teaching quality policy. The paper proposes evidence-based reforms, drawing on England's Early Career Framework (ECF), which provides detailed guidance on teacher knowledge and practices like phonics, unlike the vague Australian Standards. Professional development, aligned with revised Standards through models like instructional coaching, is essential for improving teaching quality across career stages. It recommends amending the Standards to reflect core content, conducting validity analyses, and developing national professional learning guidelines to transform the Standards into a dynamic vision of teacher professionalism.

Overview

Australian student performance has steadily declined over two decades, with PISA results showing downward trends in mathematics, reading, and science, lagging behind the OECD average. NAPLAN data highlight that many students' writing skills, including sentence structure and punctuation, are two years behind peers. Classroom climates, marked by distractions from peers and lax digital device policies, exceed OECD averages for unfavourable learning environments. Despite federal funding to address teacher deficits in classroom management, teacher unions resist linking remuneration to student outcomes, prioritising class size reductions, even though salaries rose 15% in real terms from 2010 to 2022. Policymakers pursue reforms through the National Teacher Workforce Action Plan, with the *Strong Beginnings* report (June 2023) mandating core content in ITE. Supported by $7.1 million in federal funding, these reforms aim for consistency by 2025, but the current Standards, incompatible with *Strong Beginnings*, lack guidance for professional growth, functioning as compliance tools rather than standards of quality.

What are the Professional Standards for Teachers?

Developed by the Australian Institute for Teaching and School Leadership (AITSL) in 2013, the Standards serve to assess teaching eligibility, accredit teachers at various career stages, guide ITE content, and ensure professional learning for registration. Originating from the 1998 Senate inquiry *A Class Act*, influenced by global trends and scholars like Linda Darling-Hammond and John Hattie, the Standards aimed to address underachievement. However, the 2008 Melbourne Declaration's focus on global economic readiness led to an emphasis on individualism and technology, neglecting how students learn. The 2014 TEMAG report hastened ITE alignment, but the Standards remain unchanged, outdated by post-COVID educational shifts. Intended to set "external norms", they promised to define good teaching but embraced relativism, avoiding standardised practice. A 2015 evaluation by Stephen Dinham highlighted the need for clear goals and technical knowledge, yet a 2020 AITSL review reinforced technology and learner diversity, ignoring the Science of Learning. The Standards' role in policy and accreditation underscores the need for evidence-based reform.

What evidence should inform teachers' standards?

Developing standards involves diverse stakeholders — researchers, government, unions, and parents — raising questions about influence and alignment with evidence. While Linda Darling-Hammond linked teacher traits to achievement, correlation does not imply causation, necessitating a research-based approach. Process-product studies by Brophy, Good, and Rosenshine show that high-paced, structured teaching with high success rates enhances achievement. Rosenshine's findings advocate presenting material in small chunks, checking understanding, and regular review. Andrew Martin's load reduction instruction model, grounded in cognitive load theory, guides students from novice to expert through structured practice and autonomy support, validated by student and teacher reports. North Carolina's teacher rubrics demonstrate predictive validity, linking teacher behaviours to student outcomes, unlike the unvalidated Australian Standards. Standards must have predictive power, measuring intended behaviours and correlating with student progress, particularly in subject-specific pedagogy and planning.

How the Standards fall short of the evidence

The *Strong Beginnings* core content shifts from progressive ITE models, prioritising evidence-based practices like cognitive load theory, explicit instruction, and phonics, countering misconceptions about learning. It de-emphasises differentiation, advocating whole-class instruction with responsive teaching to reduce workload. In contrast, Standard 1 overemphasises differentiation, implying diverse learning needs across groups, including socio-economic ones. Standards 1.5 and 1.6 redundantly focus on personalising learning, reflecting Melbourne and Mparntwe Declarations' priorities. Standard 1.2 vaguely references "how students learn," ignoring proven practices. The Standards' emphasis on individual curriculum writing, deemed burdensome by the Grattan Institute, lacks guidance on effective sequencing, assuming tacit knowledge. Outdated ICT references (Standards 2.6, 3.4, 4.5) and minimal attention to classroom management, linked to teacher attrition, highlight their inadequacies. Without a hierarchy of importance, universities interpret Standards variably, leading to inconsistent ITE provision.

How the Standards Could Support Teacher Workforce Needs

The Standards' limitations are amplified in the Highly Accomplished and Lead Teacher (HALT) accreditation, which prioritises "innovative practice" over practical leadership roles, hindering recognition of specialists like instructional coaches. With only 1,000 HALTs accredited by 2022, the process fails to meet workforce goals. The paper proposes domain-specific standards to recognise roles like Master Teachers, addressing rural teacher shortages through technology-supported coaching. The Standards' focus on individual curriculum design, a uniquely Australian burden, contrasts with collaborative models like Ochre Education's shared resources, which benefit remote schools. Reducing this focus could improve retention and prioritise instruction.

What Role Does Teacher Preparation Play in Reinforcing the Standards?

ITE programs must align with Graduate Teacher Standards, but numerous providers — unlike Singapore's single provider — complicate quality control. The Standards' implicit knowledge requirements, drawn from educational psychology, allow universities to prioritise sociological critiques over practical skills. *Strong Beginnings* specifies core content to maximise student learning, but providers resist, claiming they already teach it while opposing its principles. Inconsistent professional placements leave preservice teachers without shared quality teaching understanding with mentors. Without revised Standards, ITE reforms risk stagnation, as improving the workforce through ITE alone could take 28 years. Revised Standards must support graduates and professional development across career stages.

What Role Does Professional Development Play in Supporting Quality Teaching?

Effective professional development, per Sims et al., balances theoretical insights, practice goals, practical models, and practice time. Instructional coaching, like the UK's Ambition Institute and Steplab models, supports teachers through observation, feedback, and skill practice, prioritising classroom management. In contrast, Quality Teaching Rounds, despite investment, relies on subjective criteria and is time-intensive. Yates Avenue Public School exemplifies success, using explicit teaching, daily reviews, and coaching to achieve 84% of students in top NAPLAN mathematics bands by 2023. System-wide efforts in Canberra-Goulburn and Melbourne dioceses align professional development with core content, demonstrating scalability. The paper proposes national guidelines with case studies to embed these models.

What do Best Examples of Standards in Practice Suggest for Policymakers?

Mapping *Strong Beginnings* core content to existing Standards risks selective interpretation, limiting benefits to new graduates. Without amendments, mentors may struggle to support preservice teachers due to variable ITE quality. International standards, like North Carolina's and Mississippi's, share the Australian Standards' vague focus on 21st-century skills, while Singapore's TE21 allows excessive pedagogical flexibility. England's ECF, endorsed by the Education Endowment Foundation, provides concise, evidence-based guidance, integrating practical strategies like phonics and content balancing, unlike the HALT process's cumbersome documentation. The paper recommends adopting the ECF's approach for Australian reforms.

What Should We do in Australia to Better Match Our Standards to Evidence and Best Practice?

Standards 1–5 should be retained but remove focus areas, aligning them with *Strong Beginnings* core content. Standard 1 should incorporate cognitive science and responsive teaching, reducing differentiation.

Standard 2 should emphasise phonics and mathematical fluency, prioritising collaborative curriculum approaches. Standard 3 should focus on high expectations and evidence-based pedagogies. Standard 4 should centre on classroom management, and Standard 5 on formative assessment to reduce workload. Standards 6 and 7 should merge into a single Professional Engagement standard. The paper recommends factor and value-added analyses for validity and national professional learning guidelines with case studies.

Conclusions

Without revising the Standards, *Strong Beginnings* reforms risk tokenistic implementation due to university resistance. The current Standards' lack of qualitative support and evidence neutrality undermines their policy role. By integrating *Strong Beginnings* core content and emulating the ECF's clarity, Standards would guide ITE and teacher development. These reforms require vertical integration with professional development to support early career teachers and align practice with research for strong student outcomes. Amending the Standards, validating them through analysis, and developing professional learning guidelines will transform them into a living vision of teacher professionalism.

> This is a summary of a Centre for Independent Studies research paper. The full paper can be found at https://www.cis.org.au/publication/reimagining-teacher-professionalism-why-standards-must-be-part-of-ite-reform/

SECTION 2

Equity, Performance, and Accountability in Schools: What Gets Measured — and What Must Be Done

For years, the Australian education system has supported fairness as a principle, but less so in fairness as a practice. The idea of an Australian 'fair go' is often invoked, but as Matthew Taylor and Robert Breunig show in *Why We Need to Track Intergenerational School Performance*, this foundational ideal has not been matched by a rigorous effort to measure, understand, and improve educational mobility. Australia's school reforms have been heavy on funding — $319 billion since 2018 — but light on demonstrable progress. Without better data, they argue, we risk wasting billions more. Their chapter, and the others in this section, examine not just how well students are doing, but whether our systems are designed to help them do better, particularly those most at risk of falling behind.

Trisha Jha's *Lifting NAPLAN Results* cuts through the annual hand-wringing about poor performance to highlight what improves student outcomes: structured literacy, explicit teaching, and a coherent, knowledge-rich curriculum. She points out that achievement gaps—especially for students in rural areas or from less-educated families — will not be closed by wishful thinking or more money alone. The gaps will only close when schools focus relentlessly on what works.

Of course, understanding what works depends on measuring it. In *Learning Lessons: The Future of Small Group Tutoring*, Jha warns against viewing targeted tutoring as a silver bullet. She shows that tutoring, while promising in theory, falters in practice without the systemic foundation provided by a Multi-Tiered System of Supports. The lesson is simple but often ignored: no new intervention can succeed without robust classroom teaching.

The same theme runs through Glenn Fahey's *Mathematics Requires Explicit Instruction*. Fahey dissects the persistent underperformance of well-funded public systems, such as the Australian Capital Territory, and praises the quiet revolution occurring in some Catholic schools that have embraced explicit instruction. His argument, echoed in *Through High-Quality Education, Society's Inequities are Meaningfully Addressed*, is that equity is not achieved by denying differences in student background, but by confronting those differences with high expectations, excellent teaching, and early intervention.

Fahey skewers the mistaken belief that inequities in education merely reflect larger social forces that schools can't overcome. He argues, it's education that can change society, not the other way around. That claim is backed by international evidence, but it is often obscured in local debates by an overemphasis on resourcing and a reluctance to name underperformance.

Across these pieces, the theme is not that Australia lacks good intentions or even good ideas. It is that we have too often confused goals with methods. The belief that equity requires softness — in standards, in measurement, in curriculum — is not only misguided, it is also harmful. As these writers argue, equity without rigour is just sentiment. And a "fair go" without outcomes is just theatre.

13

Why We Need to Track Intergenerational School Performance

Matthew Taylor and Robert Breunig

The notion of the 'fair go' is meant to be central to Australia's national ethos. It's not easy to define, but most of us would agree it means the chance to reach your full potential, regardless of your background. This doesn't necessarily mean equality, but it does imply social mobility, where you can do better than your parents based on merit.

Education is a major driver of social mobility, with research showing educational attainment explains up to 30 per cent of the transmission of economic advantage between parents and children. But a 2024 Productivity Commission report showed the education system is not doing well in correcting the disadvantage some students face in the classroom.

For example, Year 3 students whose parents did not finish secondary school are an average of 1.3 years behind in numeracy, compared with those whose parents have a bachelors' degree or higher. By the time these students reach Year 9, this gap widens to almost four years.

The Productivity Commission report was commissioned under the Morrison government to review the 2018 National School Reform Agreement between the federal and state governments to improve student outcomes. The deal came with $319 billion in extra funding. But after five years, the report concludes, this has so far failed to make any difference in results. Given the magnitude of the funding, this is troubling on its own. The broader implications for social mobility in Australia are even more concerning.

The commission's report highlights the need for better data on educational attainment and social mobility. This will enable better analysis of the links between the two — and ultimately more effective education policy. If policymakers don't know what works, especially for students from disadvantaged backgrounds, they will spend money on the wrong things.

As children from less educated families perform significantly worse than the children of the more educated, it is far less likely their relative economic situation in adulthood will exceed that of their parents.

Unravelling the links between education and social mobility requires longitudinal data — tracking the same individuals over decades. The best example of longitudinal data in Australia is the Household, Income and Labour Dynamics in Australia (HILDA) survey, conducted by the Melbourne Institute at the University of Melbourne.

Since 2001, HILDA has tracked a nationally representative sample of about 18,000 Australians, asking them about things such as income, employment, health and wellbeing. By surveying the same people, researchers can use this data to understand influences on people's lives over time.

The Australian Taxation Office's ALife dataset, an anonymised sample of 10 per cent of all Australian taxpayers also provides significant insight into intergenerational income mobility. By following individuals over decades, researchers can observe and compare the labour market outcomes of parents with those of their children as they grow into adults.

For example, University of Technology Sydney researchers Tomas Kennedy and Peter Siminski have used HILDA and other survey data to conclude about two-thirds of Australians aged 30-34 have higher incomes than their parents at the same age.

Australian National University researchers Nathan Deutscher and Bhashkar Mazumder have used ALife to conclude about 12 per cent of Australians born into the bottom 20 per cent of family income join the top 20 per cent between the ages of 29 and 35. If a family's wealth at birth had no bearing on a child's wealth as an adult, that number would be 20 per cent.

Deutscher has also used ALife to follow individuals over 25 years and calculate the effect of where they lived as a child on their income in adulthood. Where a child grows up has a causal impact on their adult outcomes. This typically matters most during the teenage years.

The question is how much of this relates to their school. To answer this and other questions, researchers need more comprehensive longitudinal data that enables linking things such as child-care attendance, test scores, and school choice across time and with other data sources.

One important policy initiative of the National School Reform Agreement is the introduction of a unique student identifier (USI) to track individual student performance over time. This will enable data on educational outcomes to be more easily linked with other data held by state and federal governments and provide researchers with a clearer picture of how educational outcomes shapes social, economic and health outcomes later life. However, the Productivity Commission report notes the rollout of this initiative is well behind schedule.

The USI offers more than mere standardisation. Once in place, researchers will also be better able to evaluate the impact of education policy interventions by conducting randomised control trials, similar to those used in medicine to assess the efficacy of new drugs and treatments. Such trials are crucial for assessing whether a particular education policy reform, for instance a new teaching method, has a causal impact on learning outcomes.

To date, the dearth of randomised control trials in education policy has held back the Australian education evidence base.

As noted in the University of Newcastle's Teachers and Teaching Research Centre's submission to the Productivity Commission, the use of randomised control trials in evaluating education policy is hampered by the expense of collecting data from students via surveys. Better data linkage can help solve this problem.

Building a more effective education system to support, maintain and improve social mobility requires the right tools. Without better integrated data and a more reliable education evidence base, taxpayers are far less likely to see a return on the billions being spent.

This opinion piece was originally published in *The Conversation.*

14

Lifting NAPLAN Results

Trisha Jha

Every year, the national release of National Assessment Program – Literacy and Numeracy (NAPLAN) results triggers a barrage of commentary and soul-searching around the state of education and how well it serves the next generation of Australians.

NAPLAN's annual national assessment tests the literacy and numeracy skills of students in Years 3, 5, 7, and 9 in Australian schools. This year's data confirms what we learned last year when a new scoring system and set of bands was implemented. About a third of students lack proficiency across the various domains and year levels. About one in 10 students score in the lowest band (Needs Additional Support), intended to indicate to teachers and parents that these students are at serious risk of education failure unless they're given additional support.

However, those figures are averages. The proportion of students deemed not proficient will vary across schools and regions, and students' backgrounds. Students who are male, have parents with lower levels of education, live further away from a major city or are Indigenous are far more likely to be in these bottom two bands.

It's disappointing that despite substantial political investment alongside enormous financial investment — $319 billion from 2018 to 2029 — such stark achievement gaps persist.

It's all too easy to throw up our hands and say what is needed is yet more money, or — rarely voiced out loud — for the students to just be different.

Easy, but unhelpful. Thankfully, more and more Australian schools are taking matters into their own hands and embracing high-quality teaching practices based on research and evidence. If you read a news story about how a school has 'turned around' its results — and reaped the benefits of more engaged and more capable students — you will probably find some combination of structured literacy, a knowledge-rich curriculum and explicit teaching.

Structured literacy involves explicitly teaching students the building blocks of early reading: phonics, phonemic awareness, oral language, vocabulary, comprehension and fluency. As students move into middle primary, they can not only read to learn new things, but derive meaning and pleasure from the ever-increasing variety of texts and genres they are able to access.

A knowledge-rich curriculum across the school years also contributes to wider forms of literacy. This prioritises identifying the key knowledge students require to participate and thrive in the real world, then breaking it down, sequencing it and building student knowledge gradually. It's this knowledge that is the foundation of skills like critical thinking and creativity.

We can't get students to 'think critically' about the claims made in a newspaper article, a viral TikTok video or a politician's speech unless they know something about the topic. A curriculum focused on the knowledge required to be culturally literate is vital to a vibrant and active social and civic sphere.

Explicit teaching — whether it's Barak Rosenshine's direct instruction or Hollingsworth and Ybarra's explicit direct instruction — is backed by decades of evidence as the most effective and efficient way to ensure all students attain knowledge and skills.

Explicit teaching is not just when teachers explain something for the first few minutes of the lesson before letting students 'have a go' — which often results in needing to explain the same thing a dozen times as students become more disengaged and distracted.

Instead, it's a highly responsive framework involving modelling, worked examples and checking for student understanding prior to releasing responsibility to the students. Knowledge and skills are broken into small pieces and practised — and students experience success before moving on to independent work and the next step in their learning.

Not only have these strategies been vindicated by research and evidence, they also align with the scientific evidence of how human brains learn. The science of learning emphasises our need to be taught knowledge and skills that are 'biologically secondary', and how to work around the bottleneck of our limited working memory to cement learning in our long-term memory.

All these approaches to teaching have one other important feature in common: they do not leave education success up to chance, and the educational resources students might happen to benefit from at home.

What all students need to learn — explanations, examples and demonstrations — is carefully planned behind the scenes by teachers, before they even set foot in the classroom. During the lesson, teachers check to see what students have grasped from what has been taught, and respond appropriately if they are struggling. Students are constantly responding to a variety of questions before the teacher releases responsibility. They are not left, with minimal guidance, to make sense of their learning using their own background knowledge — a strategy that inevitably rewards the haves over the have-nots.

Policymakers are, slowly but steadily, realising that what matters most in education is the practice in the classroom. Their job is to then use their authority and resources to support all teachers in all schools to meet the learning needs of all students.

A great deal of progress has been made with early literacy instruction, and the nation's two biggest school systems in New South Wales and Victoria are embracing explicit instruction — with the curriculum and lesson resourcing to support this shift.

Federal Education Minister Jason Clare has also put $16 billion of additional federal funding for schools on the table, on the condition that states embrace universal early screening in literacy and numeracy, and provide support to schools to implement interventions when screening shows students are at risk.

But systems that jump to fixing intervention — Tier 2 and 3 support — are putting the ambulance at the bottom of the cliff. Investing in universal supports, around whole-class teaching and assessment, should be the priority. Systems also have the scale power to conduct desktop and field research to find out which screening tools and which intervention programs are most effective, and provide guidance about this to schools.

Students' backgrounds undoubtedly influence their future, but that need not be the deciding factor for their success or failure. If policymakers and educators work together, they can improve outcomes where it matters most: for the students.

> This opinion piece was originally published by *EducationHQ* as Lifting NAPLAN Results: What Happens in the Classroom Matters Most.

15

Learning Lessons.
The Future of Small-Group Tutoring

Trisha Jha

Overview

During the COVID-19 pandemic, small-group tutoring emerged as a solution to address learning loss. Policymakers advocated for significant investments in tutoring programs to help students catch up, particularly disadvantaged students who were at higher risk of falling behind. Despite these efforts, the effectiveness of large-scale tutoring initiatives remains questionable.

The Better and Fairer review recommended embedding small-group tutoring within a Multi-Tiered System of Supports (MTSS) framework to address learning gaps systematically. However, the lack of a structured approach to implementing MTSS raises concerns about the efficacy of tutoring interventions. This paper examines the evidence on student achievement, the effectiveness of tutoring and MTSS frameworks, and evaluates the feasibility of applying these models in the Australian context.

The Student Achievement Problem

NAPLAN data reveals that approximately one-third of Australian students do not meet proficiency standards across various domains. Students who fall behind often remain behind, highlighting systemic challenges in addressing learning gaps. Disparities in achievement are more pronounced in regional and remote areas, where nearly half of Year 9 students struggle with reading and numeracy.

While there is limited evidence of significant learning loss due to pandemic-related disruptions, existing data underscores persistent educational inequities. These disparities suggest that small-group tutoring alone may not be sufficient to address widespread learning needs, especially when scaled nationally without proper safeguards.

Understanding Small-Group Tutoring

Small-group tutoring involves targeted support for students identified as struggling academically. Research indicates that tutoring can lead to meaningful improvements in student outcomes, particularly in primary education and literacy instruction. Effective tutoring typically involves frequent sessions, trained educators, and alignment with evidence-based teaching practices.

However, the scalability of tutoring programs faces significant barriers, including staffing shortages, inconsistent implementation, and resource constraints. Tutoring should be viewed as part of a broader MTSS framework, which provides a systematic approach to identifying and supporting students with diverse learning needs.

Small-Group Tutoring Should Fit Within a Multi-Tiered System of Supports Model

The Multi-Tiered System of Supports (MTSS) framework offers a structured approach to addressing student learning needs. MTSS includes three tiers of support: Tier 1 focuses on high-quality classroom instruction for all students; Tier 2 provides targeted interventions for students who need additional support; and Tier 3 offers intensive, individualised assistance for students with significant learning challenges.

Effective MTSS implementation requires rigorous screening, diagnostic tools, evidence-based interventions, and continuous progress monitoring. While MTSS has shown promise in improving student outcomes, its success depends on consistent application of these principles and adequate support for schools.

Barriers to Implementing Catch-Up Tutoring at Scale

Several barriers hinder the effective implementation of tutoring programs at scale:

1. **Inconsistent Quality of Instruction at Tier 1:** Variability in instructional quality affects the effectiveness of Tier 2 interventions.

2. **Lack of Access to Screening and Diagnostic Tools:** Without reliable tools, schools struggle to identify students who require additional support.

3. **Limited Availability of Evidence-Based Intervention Programs:** Many schools lack access to rigorously evaluated programs that align with best practices.

4. **Insufficient Progress Monitoring:** Effective monitoring systems are essential to evaluate the impact of interventions and adjust strategies accordingly.

These challenges highlight the need for comprehensive reforms to improve Tier 1 instruction, expand access to diagnostic tools, and promote the use of evidence-based interventions.

Policy Implications

To enhance the effectiveness of small-group tutoring and MTSS frameworks, policymakers should prioritise the following actions:

1. **Improve Tier 1 Quality and Consistency:** Invest in curriculum support and professional development to ensure high-quality instruction for all students.

2. **Enhance Screening and Diagnostic Tools:** Develop a

repertoire of assessment tools aligned with Australian standards to identify students in need of support.

3. **Promote Evidence-Based Interventions:** Conduct research to evaluate promising intervention programs and provide guidance for schools.

4. **Implement Robust Progress Monitoring:** Establish systems to track student progress and inform instructional decisions.

5. **Ensure School-Based Expertise and Coordination:** Designate personnel responsible for coordinating MTSS practices and supporting school-wide improvement efforts.

A phased approach to scaling MTSS, beginning with pilot programs and informed by evaluation, will help ensure successful implementation across diverse educational contexts.

Conclusion

Student achievement data highlights significant gaps in educational outcomes, underscoring the need for targeted interventions. While small-group tutoring holds potential, its effectiveness depends on integration within a comprehensive MTSS framework. Addressing systemic challenges, such as inconsistent Tier 1 instruction and limited access to evidence-based resources, is critical to achieving meaningful improvements in student learning.

Policymakers must adopt a preventative approach, focusing on improving instruction for all students while providing targeted support for those who need it most. By investing in curriculum, assessment tools, and professional development, Australia can build a robust educational system that supports every student's success.

> This is a summary of a Centre for Independent Studies research paper. The full paper can be found at https://www.cis.org.au/publication/learning-lessons-the-future-of-small-group-tutoring/

16

High-Quality Education Addresses Society's Inequities

Glenn Fahey

Reducing inequities is a worthy ambition in education policy and practice — but delivering a better and fairer education system doesn't require revolution; it requires skilling schools for success.

Disappointingly, our schools have struggled to consistently meet the collective aspiration of excellence and equity over recent years. On the excellence front, it's well documented in standardised testing that outcomes have been largely flat or in decline. And on the equity front, a decade of Gonski school funding has not made any dent in narrowing achievement gaps — and in some cases, inequities have worsened.

This has clearly motivated federal Education Minister Jason Clare's approach to the policy portfolio.

In setting up the current review of the national school reform agreements (where Canberra and the states agree on shared goals and funding commitments), he has stressed the objective to promote "a better and fairer education system".

This is a noble goal. Not only are educators especially motivated by a strong sense of social justice and moral purpose, but all Australians also share enthusiasm for a fair go for their children. And in a genuinely free society, education is of a high standard and gives all students — no matter their background — the chance for success.

But unfortunately, there at least three common misconceptions among some of education's equity advocates that counterproductively undermine this mission.

First, educational inequity is mistakenly viewed as a structural problem, rather than a solvable one. This is because, it's argued, that in order to fix school inequity, you must first fix society's inequities. However, this premise is fundamentally wrong, as the causation is the wrong way around. It's through high quality education that society's inequities are meaningfully addressed.

Pioneering research shows that, of all the available policy levers, education is the most potent in promoting social mobility. To this end, teachers and schools are the greatest available economic and educational equity lever, not the victims of it.

It's true that disadvantaged schools and students often face more hurdles than their more well-heeled peers. But, as Centre for Independent Studies research has documented, it's also the case that many schools and teachers routinely help students overcome the educational odds through consistent commitment to evidence-based and practical solutions.

Second, it's often claimed that, because school outcomes are unequal, this means education systems currently value the wrong things. The apparent solution, then, is to change what is measured, or don't measure anything at all.

This the equivalent of blaming the barometer for bad weather. Watering down academic standards or replacing essential literacy and numeracy with broader alternatives is counterproductive and does no favours for disadvantaged students. Not measuring or reporting on school results only masks inequities; it doesn't redress them.

In adult life and employment, there is no substitute for education in opening doors and unlocking opportunities. This is a feature of the system, not a bug, so undermining students' academic pursuits will only further entrench inequality. We must do better in raising the expectations and outcomes of students of all backgrounds, not wish away disappointing results.

Third, there can be a belief that because some students start behind, they will inevitably stay behind.

In the retail industry, there's the maxim that the customer is always right: it's not acceptable to blame a customer for their expectations and, however challenging they may be, their needs should be met. But, in education, students' backgrounds and school-entry ability can, at times, be a scapegoat.

This can underestimate the agency of teachers and schools to turn around students' academic prospects. International research shows that if disadvantaged students receive consecutive years of highly effective teaching, this can entirely eliminate the initial achievement gap with better-off students. The evidence shows that the quality and duration of effective teaching is far more impactful in turning around outcomes than increases in resourcing alone.

It's also factually wrong that the educational starting line determines the finishing line. While it's true that some students start school at a disadvantage, it's in the schooling years that gaps grow. With highly-effective teaching and early intervention, most differences in students' starting skills can feasibly be overcome.

Unfortunately, too few students catch up once they've fallen behind. But it's not because some form of crude educational determinism prevents them from doing so, it is because school and system approaches to intervention for struggling learners currently needs improvement.

All Australians want more equitable outcomes for students, and policymakers can better tilt the education system to work toward this goal. But this will require backing in best practice in schools and the capacity of teachers to lift outcomes, not resigning to the defeatism inherent in educational equity ideology.

This opinion piece was originally published by the ABC.

SECTION 3

Maths Matters
— Numeracy, Anxiety & Foundations

Australia's future as a technologically capable nation — let alone a self-declared "STEM superpower"— rests uneasily on a neglected foundation: mathematics education. The essays in this section make the case that our mathematics problem is not one of ability or budget, but of misdiagnosed priorities and missed opportunities. They call for a rededication to fundamentals — early screening, better instructional design, and psychological realism about the anxieties that drive students away from numeracy.

Several contributors emphasise the need to start early. In *Setting the Preschool Foundation for Success in Mathematics,* David C. Geary highlights how early learning experiences shape not just skills but attitudes toward mathematics. Kelly Norris, in *Screening That Counts: Why Australia Needs Universal Early Numeracy Screening,* argues for numeracy screening in Year 1, noting that current assessments either come too late or are poorly designed for early intervention. Early diagnosis of difficulties with number sense could help avoid the cycle of failure that begins in the early years and often persists.

But skills alone are not the full story. *How Maths Anxiety Could Be Holding You Back* by David C. Geary and Glenn Fahey's *What Does and Doesn't Work When it Comes to Maths Anxiety?* bring much-needed attention to the emotional toll mathematics takes on a large share of students. Particularly worrying is the gender gap — girls and women report higher anxiety levels, regardless of actual performance. Geary shows how maths anxiety activates the brain's fear centres, making avoidance a rational coping strategy — but one that closes doors to future opportunity. The solution? Gradual exposure through targeted tutoring that builds confidence and competence.

Relatedly, *Programs to Help Kids Who Fall Behind in Maths Do More Than Add Up* by Kelly Norris showcases the real gains that can be made when interventions are structured, consistent, and grounded in cognitive science.

Instruction is also the focus of *Myths That Undermine Maths Teaching*, in which Sarah Powell, Elizabeth M. Hughes, and Corey Peltier dismantle seven persistent misconceptions that continue to shape how mathematics is taught in Australian classrooms. From the overemphasis on conceptual learning to the romanticising of inquiry-based learning, the authors challenge assumptions that often masquerade as progressive reform. Drawing on rigorous research, they demonstrate that many popular ideas about teaching lack evidence — and in some cases, do harm.

A recurring theme is the tension between abstract policy goals, such as becoming an international STEM leader, and the concrete, day-to-day learning experiences that determine whether students acquire the necessary skills. *Do the Maths or We Will Never Be a STEM Superpower* by Glenn Fahey puts this bluntly: without bold changes to how we teach, test, and discuss mathematics, Australia's aspirations will remain slogans. And *Early Numeracy Screening Will Help Prevent Students from Falling Behind in Maths* by Kelly Norris and Glenn Fahey explains that systemic change must begin not in Year 9 but in Year 1—or even earlier.

If these essays share a central belief, it is this: all children can learn mathematics. But students are not all starting from the same place, nor are they equally equipped to navigate the emotional landscape of the subject. Success requires intelligent policy, competent teaching, timely support, and an end to the comforting myth that a calculator can fix what curriculum and pedagogy have broken.

17

Setting the Preschool Foundation for Success in Mathematics

David C. Geary

Introduction

Mathematics is a uniquely human and relatively recent cultural development that plays a critical role in modern life. Success in school and many careers relies heavily on early mathematical competencies, which begin forming in preschool. Children who start school behind in maths often remain behind, with long-term impacts on job prospects and income. Early quantitative knowledge, particularly number system knowledge — the understanding of number words, numerals, their magnitudes, and arithmetic operations — is foundational to school mathematics learning. This paper summarises a four-year longitudinal study tracking children from age four through first grade to identify which early competencies best predict readiness for formal maths instruction. Number system knowledge at school entry predicts not only future maths achievement but also broader economic outcomes, even after controlling for intelligence and socio-economic factors. The paper first reviews early numerical abilities in infants and preschoolers, then examines the role of the home environment, and concludes with practical implications.

Early Quantitative Competencies

A strong foundation in mathematics requires specific early competencies. The debate centres on whether intuitive quantity sense or early symbolic knowledge is more critical. Both likely contribute, but symbolic knowledge appears to be the stronger predictor of school success.

Intuitive Sense of Quantity

The approximate number system (ANS) enables humans and other animals to compare quantities without counting, based on ratio rather than absolute difference. Infants and preschoolers can use this system, and it may initially help in learning number words. However, while ANS training can improve precision in quantity discrimination, it does not lead to long-term gains in symbolic mathematics. Our research supports this conclusion: ANS acuity appears to aid early understanding of number words but becomes less relevant once children grasp their meaning.

Early Symbolic Number Knowledge

Symbolic understanding, including knowledge of the count sequence, numeral recognition, and the cardinal meaning of number words, is essential for later maths learning. The key early predictor of later maths achievement is cardinal knowledge — understanding that a number word refers to a specific quantity. Acquiring this is a gradual process, typically assessed using the 'give-a-number' task. Children become 'one-knowers', then progress to understanding higher numbers, eventually gaining insight into the cardinal principle (that each number in the count list represents a unique, sequentially increasing quantity).

In our longitudinal study of children from diverse backgrounds, those who began preschool with knowledge of the count sequence, numeral recognition, and strong cardinal understanding had higher mathematics achievement by the end of preschool. The difference was substantial: most one-knowers (i.e., they did not understand the quantities represented by number words greater than one) lagged significantly behind their cardinal-principle-knower peers. In fact, beginning-of-preschool cardinal knowledge accounted for nearly half the variation in preschool maths achievement. More importantly, it strongly predicted number system knowledge in first grade — a key indicator of later employability and wages.

Timing and Long-Term Impacts

We investigated whether the age at which children became cardinal principle knowers influenced later outcomes. The results showed that earlier acquisition (before or during the first year of preschool) led to significantly stronger number system knowledge in first grade. About 10% of children had not achieved this insight by the end of preschool, and these children were at high risk of poor school readiness in maths. Importantly, this delay affected only maths, not reading skills, suggesting a specific developmental trajectory.

We hypothesised that early achievers had more time to build number system knowledge. This was confirmed by comparing their growth in numeral comparison skills (e.g., identifying which numeral is larger) with their ANS skills. Numeral comparison improved rapidly after achieving cardinal principle understanding, regardless of when this occurred, while ANS performance showed smaller gains. Early cardinal knowledge allowed for a longer period of growth in symbolic number understanding, leading to better preparedness for formal instruction.

Our final study focused on what predicts the age at which children become cardinal principle knowers. Factors included age, counting ability (enumeration), ANS acuity, numeral and letter recognition, intelligence, and executive functions. Early achievers had longer count lists (i.e., counting "one, two, three…"), better numeral recognition, and higher cognitive scores. Children who did not reach cardinal knowledge by the end of preschool often had minimal exposure to numbers or letters at home and scored lower in executive functioning. These findings highlight the importance of early exposure to number activities and the cognitive ability to sustain attention and shift between tasks.

Our studies suggest that achieving cardinal principle understanding before age 4½ is a strong predictor of school readiness in maths. This early milestone sets the stage for developing number system knowledge, which in turn underpins formal mathematics learning and long-term academic and economic outcomes. Supporting children's early counting, encouraging numeral recognition, and fostering focused attention can help more children achieve this crucial developmental goal.

Home Environment

The home environment contributes to early differences in children's number knowledge, such as reciting the count list, enumerating objects, and understanding cardinality. However, the link between home experiences and these skills is not straightforward. Cardinality is a cognitively advanced concept, unlikely to be acquired through everyday parent-child interactions, which are typically geared towards passing on cultural norms and practical activities.

Parents tend to engage children in instrumental tasks, such as counting objects or reciting number words, rather than explicitly teaching abstract concepts like cardinality. Observational studies confirm that most parent-child number activities are basic and do not reliably predict later mathematical achievement. However, when parents engage in more advanced interactions — such as comparing quantities or discussing numerical concepts — positive effects on children's higher-level number knowledge are observed.

Research suggests that the quality, not merely the quantity, of number talk matters. Activities that involve explaining or reflecting on the meaning of number words promote more complex understanding, although this kind of engagement is relatively rare and often dependent on parents' intentional efforts. Still, existing evidence is limited by small sample sizes and a lack of comprehensive data on parental knowledge and other influencing factors. Future research should clarify which types of interactions, parental traits, and child characteristics best support early number development, particularly cardinal knowledge.

Implications

These findings indicate the need for early intervention for children at risk of persistent difficulties with mathematics. While general preschool maths programmes have shown short-term benefits, their impact often diminishes over time. Providing extended or repeated versions of such interventions may help sustain gains, though this requires further testing.

Evidence from other domains, such as behavioural therapy for at-risk youth, suggests that multisystemic interventions — involving the child, family, and school environment — are more effective long term. Similarly, improving early maths outcomes may require a coordinated approach across multiple settings.

In addition to broad interventions, targeted strategies that support counting, enumeration, and understanding of cardinality may be effective. However, their success likely depends on identifying the specific classroom practices, home interactions, and child-specific traits, such as attentional control, that foster these competencies. A successful intervention strategy would address all these areas simultaneously

Conclusions

Although much is known about infants' and toddlers' early number abilities, the connection between these skills and readiness for formal maths instruction is not fully understood. However, by age 3½ to 4, children's performance on basic counting, enumeration, and cardinality tasks can reliably indicate their risk of starting school behind in mathematics. A particularly useful tool is the give-a-number task (e.g., asking a child to hand you three toys and determining if they hand you three and only three toys), which reveals how well children understand the numerical meaning of number words. Children who cannot demonstrate this understanding — often those identified as one- or two-knowers — are especially vulnerable.

Performance on these tasks correlates with standardised preschool maths tests, but they provide more precise insight into the specific knowledge gaps that need addressing. Nonetheless, we still lack a comprehensive understanding of how home life, classroom experiences, and individual traits interact to shape early number learning. Gaining this understanding will be crucial for designing effective interventions for children at risk of long-term struggles in mathematics.

> This is a summary of a Centre for Independent Studies research paper. The full paper can be found at https://www.cis.org.au/publication/setting-the-preschool-foundation-for-success-in-mathematics/

18

Screening That Counts: Why Australia Needs Universal Early Numeracy Screening

Kelly Norris

(Please note: This was a significant research report and was impossible to wholly reduce to a short summary for the purposes of this anthology. Therefore we have included the executive summary and some of the key highlights from the full report. Ed)

Better early identification of students struggling with mathematics is a critical step in addressing underachievement

Evidence shows virtually all students can reach proficiency in mathematics, if they receive systematic and high-quality instruction. But data from national and international testing shows too many Australian students are not meeting proficiency benchmarks. Those who fall behind often do so early in their school experience and rarely catch up.

Successive reviews have advocated for better assessment tools for early identification of students at risk and subsequent intervention. In particular, screening tools that are administered to all students can 'flag' students who are at-risk of later difficulties with mathematics without additional support. For students needing additional support, the chances of positive outcomes are significantly higher when intervention is early and evidence-based.

For intervention outcomes to be improved, a universal and systematic approach is needed for the early years of school. Effective early maths screening — particularly through a universal numeracy screener in Year 1 — could improve the opportunity for Australian students to be confident and successful in the subject.

Effective early screening measures should focus on robust models of number sense

There are several early markers of students' likelihood to experience difficulty in mathematics, including malleable skills such as 'number sense'.

Number sense represents a body of core knowledge about whole numbers, which predicts mathematics achievement and underlies the development of more complex mathematical skills and knowledge. Number sense encompasses the three domains of number (including saying, reading, and writing numbers), number relations (comparing and understanding numbers in terms of 'more' and 'less') and number operations (understanding and facility with addition and subtraction).

Number sense is 'teachable' and students who receive quality early interventions in number sense can experience significant and lasting benefits.

However, awareness of, and screening for, these key foundational skills is not systematically implemented in Australian schools. This means students at risk are not consistently identified early enough to maximise their chance of success.

Current student assessments in Australia do not meet adequate standards for universal screening

Evidence shows effective maths screening approaches have some characteristics in common. Mathematics screeners must be efficient, reliable and directly inform teaching practice. Importantly, they must be designed to reflect research about the skills and knowledge that are most predictive of future maths success, so the right children are identified for additional support. Screening tools must classify children as 'at-risk' or 'not at-risk' with acceptable accuracy to enable support to be appropriately allocated to where it is needed.

However, current approaches to early mathematics assessment do not represent an efficient or effective approach to 'screening'. Tools currently in use are largely diagnostic in nature or measure achievement rather than risk. Such tools are important within a broad approach to assessment but were not designed and are not suitable for screening purposes.

The Year 1 Number Check, developed in response to previous recommendations for a consistent screening tool based on number sense in Year 1, is not widely used or fit for purpose in its current form. A new or significantly redesigned tool is needed which accurately represents the skills with predictive value in Year 1, is based on a robust model of what constitutes 'number sense,' and which measures not only knowledge and strategies but fluency with that knowledge. This tool should be research-validated to ensure its accuracy in identifying risk.

Policymakers should take action to widely implement effective screening and intervention

Policy makers should implement a research-validated, nationally-consistent screening tool which measures aspects of the three domains of 'number sense,' consistent with the established research base.

Screening tools designed on a conceptual model of 'number sense' should be developed for both Foundation and Year 1, and implemented with all students at least two times per year (beginning and middle of year).

The second testing period in Year 1 should be consistent across all Australian schools and used for central data collection.

A final testing period towards the end of Term 4 should involve a standardised test of maths achievement. This can help schools to evaluate how successful the teaching program has been and track students' progress over time as they move through Primary School.

Teachers and schools should be supported with professional learning programs to enable more intensive teaching for at-risk students. Systems should provide access to evidence-based tools for intervention, and the resources with which to deliver these to students identified through screening.

Maths screening should occur within a multi-tiered framework which includes systematic processes for assessment and instruction at three tiers. Existing tools should be realigned to this framework, and progress monitoring tools developed.

Early screening and intervention is necessary but not sufficient for some students to maintain pace with grade-level curriculum. Systematic screening and intervention resources and processes are also needed for middle and upper grades.

International data have repeatedly shown many Australian school students struggle with mathematics

Around 10% of Australian students perform below proficiency levels in numeracy (NAPLAN, TIMSS), equating to ~400,000 students annually. Over 25% of 15-year-olds are low performers in maths (PISA 2022). Despite high per-student spending (23% above OECD average) and significant instructional time, achievement has stagnated or declined.

Students who struggle with maths can be identified early

Early numeracy gaps persist, with disadvantaged students entering school behind peers. Maths proficiency by Year 5 predicts future academic and life outcomes (employment, income, health). Early difficulties often lead to maths anxiety and disengagement, particularly among girls.

Lack of access to high-quality universal early numeracy screening

Current tools (e.g., NAPLAN) identify struggles too late. A nationally consistent screening tool was recommended in 2017 but remains unimplemented. Existing assessments are inefficient and not designed for universal screening.

Intervention outcomes have been mixed

Despite funding (e.g., COVID-19 tutoring programs), interventions lack reliable screening to target support effectively. Early identification and evidence-based interventions are critical to alter long-term achievement trajectories.

The role of early mathematics screening

Early screening and intervention improve achievement, reduce anxiety, and increase motivation. Success in foundational maths skills prevents a cycle of failure, particularly for girls who disproportionately avoid STEM due to maths anxiety.

What tools are Australian schools using?

Schools rely on time-consuming individual interviews (e.g., MAI, ENI) and standardised tests (e.g., PAT Maths). These are diagnostic rather than screening-focused, lack efficiency, and do not systematically predict risk.

Methods for early and universal maths screening

Universal screening, unlike diagnostic assessment, identifies at-risk students early. A **Multi-Tiered System of Support (MTSS)** framework is recommended, integrating screening, targeted intervention, and progress monitoring.

Existing early screening approaches based on Number Sense

Overseas tools (e.g., Number Sense Screener) focus on **number, number relations, and number operations**—key predictors of later achievement. Australian schools lack comparable validated tools.

Characteristics of effective screeners

Effective screeners must be:

- **Reliable** (consistent results)
- **Predictive** (linked to future achievement)
- **Accurate** (minimise false positives/negatives)
- **Efficient** (quick to administer)
- **Actionable** (clear decision rules for intervention)

Gated screening (multiple assessment stages) improves accuracy by refining risk identification.

Two main schools of thought in predicting early numeracy success

1. **Cognitive psychology**: Focuses on core deficits (e.g., symbolic number processing, mental number line).
2. **Behavioural psychology**: Emphasises measurable skills (e.g., fluency in arithmetic).

Both agree on the importance of **number sense** (number, relations, operations) for early screening.

Measuring aspects of 'number sense' in the early years of primary school

- **Number**: Counting, numeral recognition, subitising.
- **Number relations**: Comparing quantities, mental number line.
- **Number operations**: Addition/subtraction fluency.
  Skills vary in predictive power by age (e.g., counting matters more in Foundation, arithmetic in Year 1).

General considerations for universal maths screening

- **Composite measures** (multi-skill) are preferable for instructional relevance.

- **Fluency** (speed + accuracy) is more sensitive than accuracy alone.
- **Timed tasks** better differentiate struggling students.

How well do current tools fit criteria as screening measures?

Tool Type	Reliability	Predictive Validity	Efficiency	Actionability
Interviews (e.g., MAI)	Moderate (depends on interviewer)	Partial (not designed for screening)	Low (time-consuming)	Limited (no clear decision rules)
Standardised Tests (e.g., PAT Maths)	High	Moderate (broad focus)	Moderate	Low (broad, not targeted)

The role of general educational risk factors

Cognitive traits (working memory, attention) and socioeconomic status influence risk but are not practical screening targets. Focus should remain on teachable maths-specific skills.

Implications for policy and practice

1. **Implement a nationally consistent screening tool** for Year 1 (extendable to Foundation), focusing on number sense.
2. **Adopt an MTSS framework** to align screening, intervention, and progress monitoring.
3. **Streamline assessments**: Use efficient screeners universally, reserve interviews for diagnostics.
4. **Provide teacher training** on evidence-based interventions and progress monitoring.
5. **Invest in structured intervention programs** to address identified gaps.

Conclusion

Australian schools lack efficient, evidence-based screening tools for early numeracy difficulties. A coordinated approach—combining universal screening, MTSS, and targeted interventions—is urgently needed to improve long-term outcomes for struggling students.

This is a summary of a Centre for Independent Studies research paper. The full paper can be found at https://www.cis.org.au/publication/screening-that-counts-why-australia-needs-universal-early-numeracy-screening/

19

How Maths Anxiety Could Be Holding You Back

David C. Geary

The mathematical competencies of students have a long-term influence on their employability and wages in adulthood, and on their ability to navigate the many quantitative demands of day-to-day life in the modern world. These competencies are especially important for employment in many science, technology, engineering, and mathematics (STEM) fields.

However, as many as a third of Australian adults and children are affected by maths anxiety – a fear or apprehension of mathematical activities — that severely limits their employment opportunities in STEM industries.

Girls and women have higher levels of maths anxiety, on average, than do boys and men — independent of their mathematics achievement — making it yet another hurdle for increasing female participation in STEM careers.

According to the OECD's Programme for International Student Assessment (PISA) study of 15-year-old students, a one-point increase in its Index of Mathematics Anxiety is associated with a decrease in mathematics achievement of 18 score points (close to the equivalent of one year's worth of learning) after accounting for socio-economic backgrounds.

Successive PISA studies have identified increasing levels of maths anxiety among students over recent decades, pointing to compromised maths development and subsequently reduced career opportunities.

Once formed, mathematics anxiety is associated with the avoidance (to the extent possible) of mathematical activities (e.g., reduced course taking) and, through this, compromised mathematical development.

Mathematics anxiety can also disrupt performance during mathematical activities, potentially through concerns about performance that, in turn, reduces attentional resources from the mathematics learning or performance (e.g., test) episode.

It would be unwise to try and dismiss the anxiety as not being 'real'. Brain imaging studies indicate that high levels of mathematics anxiety are associated with strong reactivity of the brain network that underlies acquired or learned fears — and thus student reports of mathematics anxiety should be considered realistic appraisals of their apprehension of mathematics.

In other words, the engagement of brain regions associated with fear and anxiety reactions and ruminations about them indicate that mathematics anxiety is a real phenomenon rooted in biological systems that evolved to reduce exposure to potential threats.

The presence of maths anxiety among Australian students has prompted educators and policymakers to make adjustments in how maths is taught in efforts to accommodate or alleviate maths anxiety.

In some instances, this has resulted in calls to reduce the type and format of testing (such as relaxing the timed conditions of maths tests), reducing the emphasis on procedural understanding, and relaxing the apparent inflexibility of requiring 'correct' results to maths problems.

Many people cope with acquired fears — including mathematics anxiety — by avoiding the situations associated with the fear or anxiety, and this avoidance perpetuates it. Avoidance of mathematics will reduce long-term educational and occupational options, and thus reductions in anxiety could be beneficial for many students. The field is in the early stages of developing interventions for mathematics anxiety, but there are some promising approaches.

A common approach to the general treatment of fears and phobias is to increase exposure to the threat, which over time can result in a decline in the associated fear or anxiety. For mathematics this would involve improving basic mathematics competencies, starting at a level that would ensure success, which has been found to reduce mathematics anxiety.

This was evidenced in a study where primary school children who were highly maths anxious and their low-anxious peers participated in an eight week (three 45-minute sessions/week) one-on-one tutoring session focused on basic arithmetic.

Participants were given a brain imaging assessment before and after tutoring. The math-anxious students showed significant reductions in mathematics anxiety and both groups experienced improved basic arithmetic skills. One-on-one tutoring with adults or peers that improves mathematics competencies, is also a promising approach.

Such interventions that can limit maths anxiety, and although there is no current consensus on what is the most appropriate, these educational approaches are likely to work best if they are organised and structured in a step-by-step manner.

Academic competencies at the end of schooling are proven to influence employability, wages, and the ability to navigate the complexities of living in a developed economy. Addressing maths anxiety is key to improving the chances of success for those who suffer from it.

This opinion piece was originally published by the *Canberra Times*.

20

What Does and Doesn't Work When it Comes to Maths Anxiety?

Glenn Fahey

Rising levels of 'maths anxiety' should worry educators and policymakers. But misinformation about the issue means that many of the supposed fixes to this problem are making the situation worse.

As explained in new CIS research by eminent professor David C. Geary, maths anxiety is essentially a fear of, or apprehension about, doing maths. It's a genuine and very real condition that develops in similar ways to other widely-held fears and phobias.

The condition affects many Australian school students — and adults too. The 2017 Westpac Numeracy Study found around one in three Australians are affected by it, and high levels of distress about maths affects around one in 20.

Unsurprisingly, anxiety about maths can be linked to poor academic results. In the latest OECD-run Programme for International Student Assessment (PISA), 15-year-old students who reported relatively high levels of maths anxiety lagged the equivalent of almost a full year behind their peers.

Importantly, school students who experience maths anxiety are far less likely to be able to go on to study and work in STEM fields. But despite its prevalence and impact, maths anxiety is often poorly understood by educators and policymakers. This is largely because many conventional views on the topic are misinformed, and not supported by educational science.

First, maths anxiety is not innate; it is acquired (often from others). It's true that many claim to 'not be a maths person', in part citing their discomfort with doing maths. In turn, it's implied that some (disproportionately, girls) are simply born with inherent risk of maths anxiety.

But it is scientifically unfounded that any humans cannot be a 'maths person'. Even individuals with specific learning difficulties in mathematics — such as dyscalculia or dysgraphia — are capable, with the right support, of performing well and confidently in maths. It's generally the adults in a child's life that contribute most to maths anxiety — through either parents or teachers who themselves struggle with maths — rather than an underlying condition.

Second, maths anxiety is generally the *result* of poor achievement, not the *cause* of it. Unfortunately, this is a classic case of confusing cause and effect. It may once have been a plausible theory that some underlying anxiety about maths could be primarily responsible for poor achievement, but this has now been disproved. The research shows it is students who struggle early with maths who are much more prone to anxiety about it later in their schooling — and potentially into adulthood — rather than the other way around. Put simply, early success in maths is the best protection against maths anxiety.

Third, timed testing does not cause maths anxiety. It's true that maths-anxious students may be nervous about maths quizzes, exams, and assignments, especially when placed under some time pressure.

But this does not mean that taking away testing — including with time limits — will ultimately benefit a student. Building maths fluency is best achieved by practice that requires fast and accurate responses. And greater fluency significantly reduces — rather than exacerbates — maths anxiety.

When students can do basic arithmetic with immediate and accurate recall unconsciously, it reduces the cognitive demands when performing related tasks or problems. This is essential to improving confidence and, as a result, commitment to timed assessments actually reduces risks of maths anxiety. Further, student-led approaches will exacerbate the experience of maths anxiety.

Many student-led approaches to learning are popular in maths education — often centred around students' own personal discovery and application of mathematical concepts, experimenting with different ways to solve problems, or working on problems among groups of peers. However, some approaches of this kind are particularly ineffective for students who experience maths anxiety, because the brain's response to anxiety significantly limits the ability to inhibit irrelevant information and focus on the task.

This especially impairs maths performance in tasks that are inquiry-heavy; as evidence shows that such tasks already significantly draw on severely limited available attention, compared to more direct instructional strategies. So it's unsurprising that intervention research shows the best bet to meaningfully address maths anxiety is through direct instruction, particularly in intensive dosages in small-group settings.

Finally, while a so-called 'growth mindset framework' is sometimes claimed to be a fix for maths-anxious students, it will not in fact treat maths anxiety. A range of strategies are associated with this approach, but arguably the most controversial is the mistaken idea that failure is a brain-growing educational experience. This is simply untrue. Failure can be deeply demotivating and adversely contribute to even greater experiences of anxiety about maths. It's for this reason that carefully guided teaching and practice — where difficulty levels are purposefully staged to ensure high rates of success — are far more successful than failure-encouraging approaches.

Addressing the growing prevalence and impact of maths anxiety will be important to turning around Australia's generally declining and disappointing maths outcomes of recent decades. But the first step will be correcting the record on what works and what doesn't when it comes to maths anxiety — and ultimately in maths teaching itself.

This opinion piece was originally published by the ABC.

21

Programs to Help Kids Who Fall Behind in Maths Do More Than Add Up

Kelly Norris

Australia's education system suffers from a 'student catch-up crisis' that leaves too many children behind. Early and universal screening for educational risk is the ticket to improving these outcomes.

It is well-documented that overall levels of student achievement in Australia have generally been in decline — or at best stagnated — over recent decades. A concerning number struggle to achieve at the most basic level — with mathematics a persistent and under-appreciated weakness. Around 400,000 Australian students per year (or 10% of students) are below the lowest international benchmark in mathematics, and require additional support if they are to succeed.

Many children who perform poorly in maths in the first few years at school go on to suffer a failure cycle that can be very difficult for schools to reverse. That is because struggling to grasp the basics in the early years can trigger problems with self-esteem, motivation and anxiety. If not addressed quickly, children avoid maths, disengage in class, don't do homework, and do less practice — ultimately compounding their difficulties with maths.

Early identification of children with numeracy weaknesses can provide the opportunity for intensive, targeted intervention while the achievement gap is still small and before negative impacts on self-esteem and motivation take hold. However, the school system at large has generally disappointed in providing the education safety net needed for students who struggle. Arguably the most damning statistic in the education system is that four out of every five children who fall behind never catch up to reach proficient levels.

Improving the school system's report card on student catch-up is critical and urgent. It will take both better identifying school children at risk of falling behind and ensuring the support provided to them is early, quick, and intensive enough to turn their achievement around.

First, universal early maths screening must be done more systematically. In the health system, the population is routinely screened to identify potential risk of health conditions without waiting for adverse symptoms to appear. School systems can work in a similar way. Rather than wait for children to fail (such as in their NAPLAN tests in Year 3), early and effective screening can identify those at risk much sooner. Effective screening points teachers to where more time-intensive processes are needed, and supports them to use instructional time to maximise their impact on student learning.

Over recent years, most school systems have moved to universally screen for early reading skills, particularly the Phonics Screening Check. This brief, simple check accurately identifies which students struggle to correctly map letters, and combinations of letters, to sounds — a foundational skill that underlies learning to read. A comparable approach is also possible in maths, but requires the support of efficient, informative, accurate, and universal screening of core numeracy skills in Year 1.

Over recent years, independent reports to education ministers have highlighted the need for an evidence-based universal early numeracy screening approach to be adopted nationally, with a particular focus on Year 1. However, current approaches to assess early numeracy aren't fit for screening purposes. They require teachers to spend considerable time completing individual and detailed assessments with each child, which can result in precious class time being diverted from teaching.

Testing also doesn't focus on the right skills and knowledge that reliably predict later maths success. Less is more when it comes to universal screening — collecting only enough detail to predict risk without adding the burden of collecting information that doesn't.

Second, getting screening right is only half the equation when it comes to improving students' outcomes (after all, no one gets taller simply by being measured). Intervention too must be more effective. Once at-risk students are identified, teachers and schools need strategies and resources to deliver evidence-based, intensive support to those students and monitor their progress to see how well the intervention is working.

Over recent years, significant investment from governments has been made into school-based intervention — particularly small-group tutoring programmes introduced to address student catch-up following school closures in NSW and Victoria. Federal Education Minister Jason Clare has heavily implied that such policies could soon be scaled up and supported nationally. However, the inconvenient truth is that closing achievement gaps requires more than simply putting students into smaller groups.

Recent evaluations of the NSW and Victorian tutoring programs have shown that students receiving the extra intervention performed no better than similar students who didn't. This disappointing result is no surprise, given there's been little quality assurance to ensure gold-standard practices have been in place. For intervention to work, the right children must be identified and placed into intervention groups, as early as possible, and given the highest quality instruction. Aligning assessment to a systematic, multi-tiered framework of support is the best way to achieve this.

Good progress monitoring tools can inform agile decision-making and adjustments to ensure interventions are having the desired impact. This avoids waiting months — or years — to find precious time and resources have been misdirected into insufficiently rigorous approaches, as has been the case with NSW and Victorian tutoring initiatives.

Australia's student catch-up crisis must be addressed with improved early screening and intervention. A crucial step is to ensure that an evidence-based universal screening approach is in place for essential numeracy and reading. Time in school is a precious resource, and children are more precious still. Our teachers need the support of efficient, evidence-based tools to identify difficulties early and give every student the opportunity to be a successful student.

This opinion piece was originally published by *The Australian*.

22

Myths That Undermine Maths Teaching

Sarah Powell, Elizabeth M. Hughes, Corey Peltier

Mathematics proficiency is crucial for academic and career success, with early performance predicting future achievement. Students excelling in mathematics by age 5 tend to maintain strong performance through age 15, while early struggles can persist, particularly for students with disabilities, whose performance gaps widen over time. High-quality instruction, grounded in evidence from clinical and school-based studies, can alter these outcomes. However, myths about mathematics teaching, lacking empirical support, undermine effective practices. This paper debunks seven myths — conceptual then procedural understanding, harmful algorithms, inquiry-based learning as optimal, productive struggle's importance, growth mindset's impact, executive function training's necessity, and timed assessments causing anxiety — advocating for evidence-based instruction to enhance student success.

Maths Teaching Myth: Conceptual Then Procedural Understanding

Myth

A prevalent belief posits that students must master conceptual understanding before procedural instruction. Conceptual knowledge involves grasping concepts like number magnitude, while procedural knowledge entails steps to solve problems. This myth, possibly arising from opposition to procedural learning or resources advocating sequential learning, lacks empirical backing for improved outcomes.

Truth

Conceptual and procedural knowledge are intertwined, developing collaboratively. Studies show that conceptual instruction enhances procedural skills, and procedural practice boosts conceptual understanding. For instance, equation-solving research demonstrates that both knowledge types predict future success, with no optimal instructional order. Their bidirectional relationship suggests they are not distinct but overlapping constructs.

In Maths Teaching

To foster both knowledge types, educators should model conceptual understanding within problem-solving, such as highlighting word problem structures. Procedural steps, like solving algebraic equations, should be demonstrated explicitly. Connecting both knowledge types strengthens learning, using frameworks like concrete-representational-abstract flexibly, not sequentially. For example, teaching the Pythagorean theorem involves hands-on triangle creation alongside formula application, linking concepts and procedures.

Maths Teaching Myth: Teaching Algorithms is Harmful

Myth

Some educators believe teaching algorithms — step-by-step procedures for operations like multi-digit addition — harms students. This myth may stem from studies advocating mental strategies over algorithms or encouraging student-derived methods, but such claims lack robust evidence.

Truth

Standards emphasise teaching algorithms with conceptual understanding. Meta-analyses confirm explicit instruction, including algorithms, outperforms student-derived strategies. Research shows students using standard algorithms solve problems more accurately than those using alternatives, preferring algorithms after practice for their efficiency.

In Maths Teaching

Algorithms should be taught alongside conceptual knowledge, such as place value in addition problems. Checking students' foundational understanding ensures readiness. Explicit modelling and practice are essential, particularly for students with difficulties, who may need more repetition. Factors like maths fact fluency and working memory influence algorithm success, warranting targeted practice.

Maths Teaching Myth: Inquiry-Based Learning is the Best Approach to Introduce and Teach Mathematics

Myth

Inquiry-based learning, where students discover mathematical concepts independently, is often touted as the best method. Claims suggest it boosts achievement and curiosity, but international assessments like PISA highlight widespread maths challenges, and insufficient evidence supports these benefits.

Truth

Inquiry-based learning is less effective than explicit instruction for most students, particularly novices. Decades of research favour structured guidance over unsupported inquiry. Effective inquiry incorporates scaffolds like access to information and progress monitoring, aligning with explicit instruction's principles. Instruction should match student readiness, with explicit methods suiting beginners.

In Maths Teaching

Evidence-based practices, like explicit instruction involving modelling, practice, and feedback, should precede inquiry. Modified inquiry with scaffolds, such as guided notes or concrete manipulatives, supports success. Self-regulated strategy development (SRSD) aids multi-step problem-solving, enhancing student outcomes over unsupported inquiry.

Maths Teaching Myth: Productive Struggle is Important

Myth

Productive struggle, where students tackle complex problems to develop grit and deeper understanding, assumes challenge fosters self-regulation and motivation. However, this approach is often misinterpreted, leading to frustration rather than learning.

Truth

Excessive struggle is wasteful, not productive. Appropriate challenges require prior knowledge, which many students lack for novel problems. Explicit instruction outperforms struggle in randomised trials, supporting conceptual and procedural learning. Self-regulation needs scaffolding, with SRSD proving more effective. Motivation alone cannot compensate for skill deficits.

In Maths Teaching

Problem-solving activities should align with students' readiness and prior skills. Scaffolds, like worked examples, should be pre-planned and removable. Limited exploration (5–10 minutes) can engage students, but explicit instruction should follow. Motivation stems from skill mastery, not struggle alone.

Maths Teaching Myth: Growth Mindset Increases Achievement

Myth

Growth mindset theory posits that believing abilities are malleable enhances effort and learning. It suggests dedicating instructional time to mindset training improves maths outcomes, rooted in attribution and achievement goal theories.

Truth

Minimal evidence supports stand-alone growth mindset interventions. Studies show negligible or no maths gains from mindset training compared to skill-focused instruction. Engagement and effort are crucial, but skill development drives achievement.

In Maths Teaching

Instruction should prioritise maths skills, embedding strategies like behaviour-specific praise, self-monitoring, and goal setting to boost engagement. These low-intensity practices support persistence without diverting focus from skill acquisition.

Maths Teaching Myth: Executive Function Training is Important

Myth

Executive functions — inhibition, updating, and switching — are believed to uniquely influence maths achievement, with stand-alone training transferring to improved outcomes. This assumes targeted interventions enhance academic skills.

Truth

Executive functions correlate similarly with maths and reading achievement, not uniquely with maths. Meta-analyses show interventions improve specific skills (e.g., working memory) but do not transfer to related skills or academic outcomes. Causal links are weak due to uncontrolled variables.

In Maths Teaching

Explicit instruction minimises executive function demands by segmenting skills, using clear language, and providing practice opportunities. Visuals and manipulatives clarify concepts, while high response rates build automaticity, reducing working memory load.

Maths Teaching Myth: Timed Assessments Cause Mathematics Anxiety

Myth

Timed assessments are believed to cause maths anxiety by inducing stress, with critics arguing they prioritise speed over understanding. This myth fuels resistance to fluency-focused practices.

Truth

No causal evidence links timed assessments to anxiety. Properly implemented, they enhance fluency—speed and accuracy—critical for reducing cognitive load. Curriculum-based measurement relies on timed assessments for accurate progress monitoring. Retrieval practice under timed conditions strengthens skill automaticity.

In Maths Teaching

Timed assessments should target students' instructional range, using class median performance to guide task selection. They should be low-stakes, avoiding grades or punitive consequences. Goal setting, like beating personal scores, motivates students. Sufficient items prevent early completion, reducing peer pressure.

Conclusion

Myths about maths teaching persist despite lacking evidence, undermining student outcomes. Debunking myths — conceptual before procedural, harmful algorithms, inquiry as optimal, productive struggle, growth mindset, executive function training, and timed assessments causing anxiety—highlights the need for evidence-based practices. Recommendations include modelling conceptual and procedural knowledge together, teaching algorithms with understanding, using explicit instruction, scaffolding struggle, focusing on skills over mindset, minimising executive function demands, and implementing low-stakes timed assessments. Adopting these practices ensures high-quality instruction, maximising student success in mathematics.

This is a summary of a Centre for Independent Studies research paper. The full paper can be found at https://www.cis.org.au/publication/myths-that-undermine-maths-teaching/

23

Early Numeracy Screening Will Help Prevent Students From Falling Behind in Maths

Kelly Norris, Glenn Fahey

Policymakers are on the verge of a major education reform — early numeracy screening — that will prevent children falling behind in their mathematical learning. NAPLAN data confirms that one in three students lack proficiency in numeracy at Year 3.

Over recent weeks, the NSW and federal governments have promoted new numeracy screening for children in Year 1. NSW Education Minister Prue Car has championed the cause and is actively considering policy solutions, while federal Education Minister Jason Clare has mandated early literacy and numeracy screening as a condition for $16 billion in funding.

This screening would help teachers to identify kids struggling early so that targeted support can be provided. Policy leadership on this will, in time, mean schools are better equipped to provide the early identification and intervention that many students need.

The unfortunate truth is that schools are generally failing on this count. Too often, early difficulties with maths become entrenched problems that persist right throughout schooling. Analysis of NAPLAN data shows that out of every five Year 3 children who fall behind, four will never go on to be proficient. While many children struggle with maths from time to time — and can be supported through general classroom instruction — some difficulties can be an early warning sign for ongoing challenges. Good screening tools help teachers to see the difference.

Australia successfully implements national programs for the early detection of various types of cancer for adults. Newborn babies are screened for hearing problems and serious illnesses. The need to screen is equally important in education — particularly given how closely risk factors in literacy and numeracy predict later socio-economic and welfare outcomes.

In reading, universal screening is becoming common practice. The Year 1 Phonics Check — now in use across most Australian states — identifies Year 1 students who are struggling with early reading by zeroing in on an essential reading skill related to decoding the letters and letter patterns in words. Where phonics screening is used widely, it results in steady improvement in literacy achievement. For numeracy screening, students might be asked to match numerals to dots, judge which of two numbers is more or solve some small number combinations.

Universal screening in education is key to greater success in the long term — just as it is in addressing health conditions early, allowing for timely intervention or treatment that can prevent complications and improve outcomes. Effective screening would ensure that follow-up support — like the 'catch-up tutoring' initiative forecast by federal minister Clare — can be offered earlier when the achievement gap is much smaller.

Although universal screening is standard in health, it's not as common in education. This is largely due to three misconceptions.

First, some think extensive school testing makes additional screening unnecessary. Schools collect a lot of data through standardised tests like NAPLAN and classroom assessments to track achievement against curriculum goals. They also use diagnostic assessments, such as one-on-one interviews, to understand students' current mathematical thinking and guide teaching. However, screening has a different purpose. It aims to identify children who might face future challenges. This helps teachers, at an early stage, address potential barriers to progress.

Second, some claim brief screening checks are not holistic enough to be useful. It's true screening checks are less detailed than other assessment types, but this is by design. By focusing only on key skills that are crucial for learning progress, educators can intervene early in areas that significantly impact a student's overall academic performance. This targeted approach can prevent small issues from becoming larger problems.

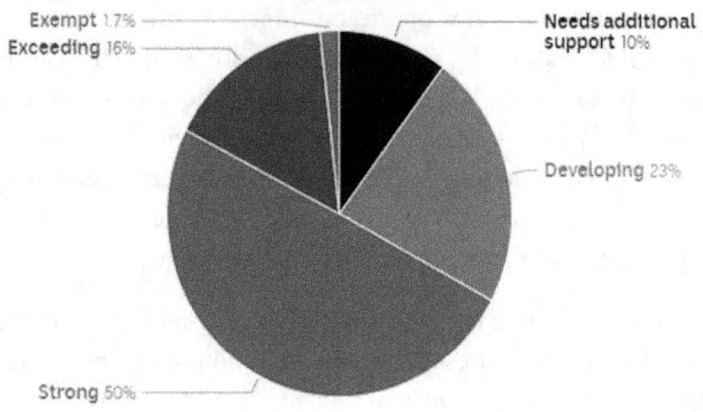

Source: Australian Curriculum, Assessment and Reporting Authority

Third, some critics are uncomfortable with any form of academic assessment for young children. They cite concerns that testing is inappropriate in a time of such rapid development, and can cause anxiety. Yes, children learn at different rates. But it doesn't follow that we should be comfortable in condemning some of them to more than 10 years of struggling in school.

Concerns that testing might cause anxiety are understandable but don't apply to screening. Screening costs little in time and effort but has the capacity to have huge benefits in the form of school success and longer-term life outcomes. Getting screening right in Australian schools is the best bet in securing the educational safety net our schools need. Top marks go to the education ministers on leading policy debate.

This opinion piece was originally published by the ABC.

24

Do the Maths or we Will Never be a STEM Superpower

Glenn Fahey

Calls for Australia to become a STEM superpower will never be answered unless our students can match the world's best in maths. However, Trends in International Mathematics and Science Study (TIMSS) results show a mixed report card in student achievement compared to benchmark countries — with four key trends apparent.

First, Australia continues to lag well behind the world's best, with 72 per cent of our 10-year-olds and 64 per cent of 14-year-olds proficient in maths — around the same level of Eastern European countries — compared to more than 90 per cent and 85 per cent respectively in the highest performing school systems (mostly concentrated in East Asia).

Second, there has been a long-term malaise in maths. Since the mid-2000s of international testing in maths, the average Australian student achievement in TIMSS has been essentially flat. The same is also found in our NAPLAN assessments. And in international tests of 15-year-olds, results have declined at among the steepest rates in the world for decades.

Third, maths performance has been poorer than in other domains. Over recent years, Australian students have recorded generally promising results in early reading. The TIMSS-equivalent in reading, the Progress in International Reading Literacy Study (PIRLS), last year showed around 80 per cent of 10-year-olds are proficient readers. At the same time, 15 years of NAPLAN data has confirmed a modest long-term improvement in reading in primary school. Similarly, in science, 83 per cent of Australian 10-year-olds in TIMSS are proficient in science — matching students in Hong Kong. And in the NAPLAN equivalent for science, performance has generally been stable over more than 15 years of domestic testing of Year 6 and Year 10 students.

But the fourth trend is that Australian students have the equal-largest maths gender gap in the world. The difference between the performance of 10-year-old boys and girls sits, with France, as the biggest globally. This gap has grown over the past decade despite girls and boys previously level–pegging in the 1990s and 2000s.

This adds up to an urgent need to raise maths achievement — particularly if Australia is to remain internationally competitive in the world of STEM. To do so will require a shift in education policy and practice. First, Australia needs a determined focus on ambitious national improvement targets.

Australia's national aspiration must be to perform at the levels of East Asia, not Eastern Europe. Yet there are currently few clear national objectives for improving education outcomes. The (nearly decade-old) National STEM School Strategy did not set an explicit achievement target. Current efforts from Federal Education Minister, Jason Clare, to embed modest national and state targets for student outcomes within funding agreements remain contested in the big Eastern states.

Second, Australia must abandon faddish approaches to STEM education and better build on maths foundations. Much STEM education is heavy on 21st century skills — trendy capabilities like creativity, collaboration, critical thinking, and the like — but lite on essential maths facts and a focus on mastering the basics.

Recent debates in Australia have foolishly questioned the role of learning basic foundations — like multiplication tables and being able to quickly compute simple equations — rather than doubling down on these skills. This is borne out in our students' results. For instance, though Australian children perform comparatively well in tasks like reading, displaying, and interpreting data, they perform less well on simple equations using fractions and whole numbers.

Third, we must abandon wrongheaded approaches to the STEM gender gap. Too many educationalists think the source of the gender gap comes from sociology rather than science. This has led to a misguided belief that lifting girls' maths results only be achieved through overcoming gendered societal norms and stereotypes.

However, it's not a lack of engagement, but a lack of achievement that's to blame for girls' underperformance. Experts on the STEM gender gap have found that, in the main, boys and girls can successfully achieve in maths, but that girls who struggle with the subject can be relatively more susceptible to suffering from anxiety with maths.

And finally, we need to enhance the size, strength, and skill of Australia's maths teachers. It's no secret that Australian classrooms have struggled to staff maths classes for decades, with persistent out-of-field teaching in the subject. When teachers themselves lack confidence in maths, this impacts their confidence teaching it. In turn, students with non-specialist maths teachers generally achieve at a lower level than their counterparts.

This challenge is not limited to high school, as Australia's primary school teachers are especially likely to lack preparation in maths during their training and to achieve at relatively low levels in maths themselves at school.

Australian policymakers and industry often talk a big game about Australia's STEM future. But this will remain compromised whilst our students lag the world's best in maths education. Without commitment and dedicated focus on maths, Australia will remain a second-rate country in STEM.

This opinion piece was originally published by *The Australian*.

25

Mathematics Requires Explicit Instruction

Glenn Fahey

Parents — and taxpayers — must wake up to the inconvenient truth that the education system has long underperformed. But there could finally be an opportunity to turn that around with the current independent inquiry into literacy and numeracy.

It might come as a surprise that the ACT's education system is the subject of scrutiny. Students' test scores are near or at the top of Australian rankings, and the school system is also the country's best funded. But several key facts should shake the longstanding comfortable complacency.

First, it's clear ACT schools significantly underperform when compared with schools with similar background-students elsewhere in the country. A 2017 report commissioned by the Directorate showed results were poorest in maths — with Year 5 students in public schools around 6 months behind comparable students in other cities. And a 2018 ANU study found ACT students were 8–12 months behind in secondary maths compared to similar schools.

Unfortunately, rather than engage with this, the government has preferred to deny it. It has rejected the way socio-educational advantages are calculated and repeatedly questioned the role of standardised testing like NAPLAN.

Second, a transformative educational improvement in the territory's Catholic schools is sharpening the divide with public schools. Canberra's Catholic schools are undergoing a unique shift in teaching practice across their system. In just a few short years, this already shows impressive indications of success.

In 2019, 56% and 74% of ACT public schools performed more poorly than similar schools in Australia for Year 3 and Year 5 numeracy respectively. In Catholic schools, this was a lower — but still alarming — 41% and 65% respectively. By 2022, the trends couldn't be starker. Across the same measures, public schools remained at 66% and 72% respectively. But the share of Catholics underperforming had effectively halved to just 17% and 35% respectively.

This shows the current inquiry is necessary, long overdue, and that there is an evidence-based path to achieve more success across the entire education system. Recent CIS research shows how the ACT could turn around its maths results by boosting maths teaching in its schools.

First, there's strong evidence on teaching practices that maths teachers can rely on. Around the world there's increasing interest in maths teaching informed by science of how children learn — referred to as the 'science of maths' movement. This research indicates what works best and what isn't effective. Sadly, many widely-held beliefs and practices are simply not supported by the best education science.

Fundamentally, maths instruction should be explicit and generally led by teachers — with step-by-step demonstrations, offering repeated opportunities to practice with guidance, and providing active and fast-paced questions from teachers.

Second, though many children show signs of struggling with maths, some supposed remedies for this problem make it worse. For some educators, parents, and even academics, the solution to poor engagement or interest in the topic, or even for conditions like 'maths anxiety', is to limit their exposure to maths. This can include replacing 'boring' maths — like arithmetic or rehearsing common 'maths facts' like multiplication tables with 'fun' maths — generally games, puzzles, and the like. But often this just means children never engage confidently with the maths they need to learn.

Similarly, because some children become anxious about maths tests under time pressure, it's tempting to reduce reliance on this kind of test or practice. But the reality is that, without requiring both quick and accurate answers from students, they won't become fluent enough to handle more complex maths as they get older. And third, focusing on early maths skills really adds up.

Though early education is generally highly valued, specific maths preparation for school is not well understood. By the time school starts, several capabilities are likely to predict how well children will do in maths throughout their schooling. The ability to count numbers in sequence, determine basic quantities (such as correctly interpreting the number of objects), and especially to consistently and correctly associate a number with a specific quantity are all key to early foundations.

Maths education has long suffered throughout the declining school outcomes over recent decades. There is an unfortunate legacy of some academics, bureaucrats, unions, and policymakers who've not only done little to improve maths teaching, but have actually contributed to this problem.

The current inquiry gives the ACT the chance to lead the nation in reforming the way it teaches, tests, and talks up maths in our classrooms.

> This opinion piece was originally published by the *Canberra Times* as Our Education System is Underperforming, But There Could be a Chance to Fix That.

SECTION 4

History, Civics, and Citizenship

If national identity is a story we tell ourselves, then education is where that story begins. This section explores how Australia teaches its young citizens to understand their history, participate in democracy, and grapple with the responsibilities of civic life. These five essays reveal a troubling gap between the aspirations of our national curriculum and the cultural and intellectual inheritance it delivers.

In *Teaching National Shame*, Joanna Williams draws attention to the corrosive effect of curricula that focus exclusively on national failures. While acknowledging the importance of reckoning with historical wrongs, she warns that an overcorrection towards guilt and grievance risks displacing the unifying power of a shared narrative. History, she argues, should cultivate understanding, not alienation.

Fiona Mueller picks up this thread in *Will Generation Lockdown Write Good History?* and *Missed Chance for Civics*. Mueller laments the marginalisation of history and civics in Australian education—a "nice to have" subject reduced to fragmented content and disconnected objectives. Her argument is not nostalgic, but civic-minded: without a coherent historical framework, students lose the ability to think analytically about the present or imagine a common future. The disjointed curriculum and lack of interest in robust civic instruction leave students adrift in a world that increasingly demands both.

In *The Argument for Debate*, Deidre Clary and Fiona Mueller shift from content to method. Debate, they argue, is not just a classroom exercise but a foundational democratic skill. It cultivates reasoned thinking, linguistic dexterity, and moral seriousness. Drawing on both ancient traditions and contemporary research, they show how structured debate improves literacy, civic awareness, and engagement, particularly for disadvantaged students. In short, debate is a proven tool for achieving the goals that the curriculum only vaguely gestures toward.

Mueller's final piece, *The Way Forward for the Australian Curriculum*, is both diagnosis and blueprint. She argues that the curriculum review process has been overly bureaucratic and philosophically timid. What's needed is not more stakeholder consultation, but a firmer intellectual spine. A national curriculum should be more than a list of competencies—it should be a framework for belonging. She calls for a return to core knowledge and a recognition of the Western heritage that undergirds our democratic institutions.

Together, these articles make the case that history and civics are not electives in the formation of a good society—they are its foundation. A nation uncertain of its past cannot prepare its citizens for the future. If we wish to preserve our democracy, we must first teach it—not just as a system of rules, but as a culture, a language, and a set of arguments we must learn to make, and to answer.

26

Teaching National Shame: History and Citizenship in the School Curriculum

Joanna Williams

Identification with a nation-state has the capacity to unite disparate individuals in a shared sense of identity and purpose, with education playing a role in the transmission of this identity through a common curriculum.

In this paper, UK analyst Joanna Williams examines the impact of changing approaches to teaching history and citizenship on the cultivation of national identity in Australia and the UK. She notes that the history curriculum has long provided a specific site for the teaching of a national story, while distinct lessons in citizenship are a more recent development.

In both countries, however, rather than celebrating national successes, history classes increasingly focus on sins of the past, thus teaching national shame. Schools have also promoted the values of global rather than national citizenship, with civics lessons encouraging local political activism as a form of democratic engagement. The legacy is cohorts of young people who have grown alienated from their nation-state and its democratic processes.

The paper concludes by calling for greater balance in the teaching of history, whilst pointing out that the very existence of formal citizenship classes speaks to a lack of confidence and consensus in the values associated with national identity. If a new generation is not to be left alienated from its collective past, the nation-building role that schools once played should be revived.

Introduction

Education has long played a role in shaping national identity, often through the hidden curriculum, traditional subjects like history and literature, and more recently, formal citizenship education. In Australia and the UK, changes to history and citizenship teaching increasingly promote critical perspectives of national narratives and a focus on global citizenship. These shifts risk alienating young people from a shared national identity, especially when activist educators interpret curriculum content through a political lens. Surveys show declining national pride, particularly among younger and left-leaning citizens, suggesting politicised teaching has influenced generational attitudes toward national identity.

Rewriting the past

How societies teach history greatly influences young people's understanding of their place within the nation. While it is essential to acknowledge historical wrongs, an excessive focus on past atrocities undermines a unifying national narrative. Recent iconoclasm reflects deeper disillusionment with national identity rather than isolated discontent with historical figures. This trend has historical roots, with educators questioning traditional values since the early 20th century. When history is used to divide rather than unite, young people are left confused, lacking a shared cultural foundation. Without consensus on what should be taught, students are exposed to fragmented content, impeding national cohesion.

Elites against the nation

Since the early 20th century, sections of the cultural elite have expressed scepticism toward the nation-state, a sentiment that intensified after World War I. In both the UK and Australia, the interwar years marked a break from the past, though in different ways. While figures like Churchill later sought to rekindle national unity during WWII, intellectuals remained critical of nationalism. This scepticism persisted into the post-war period, where elite disdain for national identity grew alongside support for global governance structures. As globalisation eroded traditional state sovereignty, notions of citizenship became increasingly fluid, with expressions of national pride often stigmatised. The promotion of cosmopolitan or European citizenship, especially through education, reflects a deliberate move to detach children from national affiliations in favour of engineered identities aligned with transnational ideals.

From pride to shame in the history classroom

The history curriculum is a powerful tool for shaping national identity, and recent decades have seen a shift from knowledge to skills-based learning. This change reflects a view that the past is open to multiple interpretations, often leading to an emphasis on emotional engagement over factual understanding. In Australia, efforts to use history for reconciliation and justice risk prioritising political goals over truth-seeking. The inclusion of emotional concepts like empathy in assessment criteria allows activist educators to influence students' views. For history to be educational rather than ideological, it must focus on rigorous knowledge and critical thinking rather than pre-determined moral lessons.

Lessons from diversifying the UK curriculum

Efforts to diversify the UK history curriculum began in the 1970s and have intensified in recent years. A focus on identity-based histories — such as black, indigenous, and women's history — has aimed to correct past exclusions but often leads to fragmented teaching and a loss of chronological understanding. Attempts by the Conservative government to restore a cohesive national story met strong resistance from the educational establishment. Despite widespread inclusion of diverse histories, public discourse continues to portray the curriculum as Eurocentric. The 2021 CRED report challenged this narrative, suggesting a more nuanced understanding of British history, yet faced backlash. Government responses propose a knowledge-rich curriculum that includes Britain's global context, aiming to temper activist interpretations. However, whether this will restore balance in classrooms remains uncertain. Ultimately, a fair historical education must give children both the critical tools and the national context necessary to form a grounded, inclusive sense of identity.

From National to Global Citizenship

Elite debates have questioned the role of schools in fostering national identity through subjects like history, instead supporting citizenship education aimed at social justice and loyalty to transnational causes. Citizenship classes now often promote local activism aligned with global values rather than allegiance to nation or family, reflecting a shift in the perceived purpose of education.

The Evolution of Citizenship Education in Australia

Australia has long included civics and citizenship education (CCE), initially to foster national unity and informed political participation following federation in 1901. However, enthusiasm for this nation-building role waned over time. A 1994 report revealed low civic knowledge, prompting the federal government's 1997 *Discovering Democracy* initiative. Despite funding and policy support, implementation varied widely due to lack of mandates. By the mid-1990s, CCE began shifting towards global citizenship, supported by the 2008 Melbourne Declaration and 2012 ACARA guidelines. Globalisation and initiatives like OECD's PISA further encouraged educators to prioritise transnational issues such as sustainability and social justice. This moral and political approach to education focuses on local action within a global framework, often at the expense of traditional, knowledge-rich content.

Linking Citizenship to Diversity in the UK

Unlike Australia, the UK historically did not teach formal citizenship, relying instead on an assumed national identity. This changed under New Labour in 1997, when citizenship classes were introduced to counteract social exclusion and political disengagement among youth. The 1998 Crick

Report called for a transformation of political culture, and citizenship was made compulsory in 2002, though implementation remained inconsistent. The 2007 Ajegbo Report linked citizenship to diversity, prompted in part by the 2005 London bombings and concerns over integration. The curriculum was revised in 2008 to stress responsible citizenship and shared identity while recognising cultural complexity. Over time, citizenship education became a catch-all response to political and social anxieties, especially post-Brexit, when there were renewed calls to use education to foster cohesion. The 2021 CRED report suggested this could best be done by engaging students with Britain's diverse cultural history through academic subjects rather than citizenship instruction alone.

The Problems with Teaching Citizenship

Global citizenship is an abstract concept that lacks the unifying power of national identity. Although intended to address democratic disengagement, it undermines the nation-state as the foundation of democracy. Unlike traditional subjects, citizenship classes often reject intellectual content in favour of community-based activism, which some students view as irrelevant or even degrading. These classes convey political agendas under the guise of universal values, often avoiding critical debate. For example, sustainability is presented as an unquestionable good rather than one of several policy approaches. This moral framing distances students from political decision-making and promotes behavioural conformity over free thought. Ultimately, the attempt to solve political alienation through education, rather than through politics itself, risks deepening disengagement and restricting students' intellectual and moral autonomy.

Conclusions

National identity offers a powerful, unifying framework that education is well-placed to nurture. A shared curriculum can transmit cultural heritage and promote critical engagement with the nation's history, both positive and negative. However, in both Australia and the UK, schools have shifted towards fragmented, theme-based learning that weakens national connection and civic engagement. Citizenship education attempts to compensate for this loss, but by directing attention away from national identity and intellectual development, it worsens the very issues it seeks to resolve. Reviving the nation-building role of education is essential if future generations are to feel rooted in their society and capable of effecting meaningful change.

This is a summary of a Centre for Independent Studies research paper. The full paper can be found at https://www.cis.org.au/publication/teaching-national-shame/

27

Will Generation Lockdown Write Good History?

Fiona Mueller

Twenty-first century history is being made each day. The news is full of statue-toppling anarchists and clueless looters, politicians making life and death decisions on COVID-19, increasing cybercrime and human rights abuses, loss of respect for longstanding international conventions of the sea and air ... and the list goes on. Language is debased, with attacks on individuals rather than the robust and respectful exchange of ideas, and it is often a struggle to see past the polemic.

At times like these, there can be a realisation of a desperate need for knowledge and skills to examine ourselves and our past to reassure ourselves that people are capable of great goodness. Only the sophisticated, inquiry-based study of human history can do this.

Downunder, reviewers of the Australian Curriculum have a tiny window of opportunity to make History the go-to subject that will finally stand tall alongside English, Mathematics and Science as signalled when those first four learning areas were prioritised back in 2011. If, as the Alice Springs (Mparntwe) Declaration states, the aim is that "All young Australians become confident and creative individuals, successful lifelong learners, and active and informed members of the community", the study of History (including Ancient, Modern and Australian) sits at the heart of the national curriculum.

Unfortunately, as with foreign languages and the arts, Australian education places History in the category of 'nice to have' but without widely accepted value 'in the real world'. This subject area also suffers from some of the same issues as STEM and languages – too few highly trained teachers, and too little public support for intellectually rigorous education.

At its very best, the study of history — more than any other area of the curriculum — produces analytical thinkers, researchers with academic integrity and deep curiosity, competent writers and thoughtful debaters who marshal the evidence to explain the past, the present and the possible future. But Australian education is reaping what we have sown — a weak, disjointed curriculum, lacking a powerful overarching national narrative (see Singapore for contrast) and clear, high standards. This is particularly evident in History, with its inconsistent delivery, small enrolments in Years 11 and 12 and minimal alignment with the separate subject of Civics and Citizenship.

Now we have pyjama-clad generations of lockdown people who will base their understanding of this period in Australian and world history only on their personal experience of the pandemic or the curated storylines of social media. Encouraging a focus on the shape of the day and a sense of belonging, some schools and systems are mandating that students appear in uniform — or at least fully dressed in appropriate clothing — when remote learning starts.

Many Australians who aren't out of their pyjamas by 9 am are in secure jobs that have easily transferred to a keyboard and earbuds away from the office. Those on the medical frontline will be too exhausted to reflect too much. Millions of others have lost their jobs or businesses and won't be terribly inspired to analyse their experience. The mums and dads who are trying to keep smiling while homeschooling children and simultaneously worrying about elderly relatives and vulnerable friends and neighbours have other priorities.

So who will write the history of these strange times? As the saying goes, those who do not remember the past are condemned to repeat it. And history does tend to be written by the winners. The revised Australian Curriculum needs to be a winner, especially in that most precious field of History.

This opinion piece was originally published by *The Spectator.*

28

Missed Chance for Civics

Fiona Mueller

The current review of the Australian Curriculum seems an almost covert operation, and neglects the pressing need to elevate Australian Civics and Citizenship. The latest CIS paper, *A 2021 Education Resolution: Keep an eye on the Australian Curriculum,* assesses the potential opportunities at risk of being neglected in the review.

Australian students and their teachers deserve the best possible curriculum, but the trajectory of the review doesn't inspire confidence. A clever country would shine a probing spotlight on this national education project, which claims to ensure the nation's ongoing economic prosperity and social cohesion.

The paper follows recently released results of the National Assessment Program – Civics and Citizenship, which revealed 62% of Australian students nearing school-leaving age didn't achieve the proficiency standard, and 87% couldn't interpret the results of a hypothetical federal election. For this reason, the review must chart a balanced approach to the nation's heritage as a Western liberal democracy and must redress a curriculum that is currently completely lacking in intellectual and cultural firepower.

There are replicable examples of curriculums that prioritise a 'love of country', particularly high-performing Singapore. Closer to home, this is also a common theme in the education and broader aspirations of Indigenous Australians but can barely be detected in the wider curriculum.

This is the time to recast Civics and Citizenship — ironically, the subject that few seem to care or know much about — as the major integrating feature of the Australian Curriculum.

Centring the curriculum around our cultural and intellectual heritage would mean a far more solid foundation, but there should also be room for schools and teachers to weave in material appropriate to local students and communities. This would help ensure students can meet the objective of becoming successful lifelong learners who can make sense of their world and think about how things have become the way they are — as the goals outline.

However, there has been no widespread public consultation to determine priorities and there is only a brief window of opportunity to comment on proposals for changes. Every Australian has a stake in this review, especially as the country works to recover from the consequences of the pandemic and position strongly for the future.

This opinion piece was originally published by the CIS *Ideas@TheCentre*.

29

The Argument for Debate: How School Debating Can Improve Academic Outcomes and Foster a Stronger Democracy

Deidre Clary, Fiona Mueller

The Education Goals for Young Australians prioritise "excellence and equity" and the formation of "active and informed members of the community". However, Australian students' well-documented decline in academic achievement (especially in the English language) has eroded public confidence. Furthermore, their inadequate understanding of the nation's governance has led to a 2024 Senate *Inquiry into civics education, engagement, and participation in Australia.*

The latest wave of Australian education reform now centres on restoring evidence-based approaches to *what* and *how* students learn. Borrowing heavily from traditional practices, and drawing on what is commonly referred to as 'the science of learning', this involves creating a "knowledge-rich curriculum" with "coherent and sequenced" content, supported by "explicit" teaching.

The so-called 21st century skills (the 4 Cs) of *communication, collaboration, critical thinking*, and creativity seem naturally aligned with the traditional practice of debating. Working either solo or as part of a team, an effective debater undertakes sound research, anticipates and responds to all possible perspectives, takes a reasoned position, and makes the case articulately and persuasively.

While the Australian Curriculum advocates the development of argumentation skills — mainly through writing — the few references to the art of debating do not reflect the evidence of its significant cognitive, linguistic, philosophical and socio-political benefits. Thus, schools and teachers are less likely to include it among their strategies for meeting curriculum requirements.

Evolving over millennia from its ancient Greek origins, debate is at the heart of Western intellectual culture. Described as "a well-known pedagogical technique since there have been written records about teaching and learning", it is a proven instrument for sustaining Western traditions that prize logic, linguistic dexterity and the robust, civil exchange of ideas. In the 21st century, debating takes many forms, from a highly structured parliamentary style to team policy, one-on-one and public forum debates. Technology allows considerable innovation. Much of the resilience of this ancient art, according to researchers, is due to "its associations with two powerful concepts: critical thinking and democracy".

The available research underscores its potential to address academic and cultural deficits in the education of young Australians. It is a proven strategy for cementing knowledge across multiple subject areas, enhancing English language proficiency and for encouraging thoughtful, articulate, confident civic engagement.

A second review of the Australian Curriculum (2021-2022) missed a crucial opportunity to prioritise citizenship and nation-building, in which debate plays a key role. In the absence of a rigorous academic framework, Australia's national curriculum lacks deep and unifying philosophical and intellectual themes. By contrast, the world's highest-performing education system — where English is the language of instruction — places a meticulous emphasis on citizenship. Singapore's national curriculum is grounded in national values.

At the time of writing, the 48th Parliament of Australia is due to be elected by May 2025. An election magnifies the challenges for politicians as they seek to defend their legislative positions. It also highlights an undervalued and arguably underused obligation of Australia's political leaders: the debate.

Federal and state/territory governments are under intense public scrutiny regarding cost-of-living pressures, energy supply, national security and defence, immigration, productivity, indigenous representation, health, education, youth crime and numerous other policy areas. Calls for open and comprehensive debate on these issues are a reminder of an ancient practice that stimulates civic participation, holds political leaders to account, and remains a cornerstone of a free and civil society. The lead-up to an election is also a timely opportunity to consider the effectiveness of the two Education Goals for Young Australians authorised by the nation's nine education ministers.

This paper places the ancient art of debate at the nexus of an impending election, rising scepticism about political leadership and decision-making, and ongoing concerns about the effectiveness of national education goals in preparing young Australians for post-school life and work in a democracy. A renewed emphasis on debating across the curriculum would raise the academic bar (especially in the English language), boost students' appreciation of Australia's Western foundations, and strengthen the nation's democratic decision-making culture.

Debating takes many forms in school contexts, including whole class, team policy, one-on-one and public forum debates. For example, a whole class debate centres on a proposition. Students research all possible perspectives and decide whether to argue for or against. A key aspect of most debating types is effective questioning used to challenge the opposition's argument. Highly structured debates generally follow the Oxford style. Australian students can choose to practise Parliamentary style debate and engage in Mock Trials among other competitions such as the NSW Premier's Debating Challenge.

Why Debate Matters

Debate is a political and intergenerational obligation in a democracy. Australian politicians have a constitutional, professional, and moral duty to engage in high-quality debate, as it is fundamental to the nation's bicameral system. Parliamentary debate allows for the expression of diverse views, shaping national aspirations and public opinion. Freedom of speech, a cornerstone of Western democracy, is enshrined in Australia's Constitution and traces back to the UK Bill of Rights (1688). Political leaders should model robust debate, fostering accountability to an informed public.

Schools must also prioritise debate to uphold democratic values and pass on essential civic skills.

An Ancient Art for 21st Century Learners

Debate has ancient origins, dating back to Greece and Rome, where philosophers like Protagoras, Socrates, Plato, and Aristotle used it to explore ethics, justice, and governance. Socrates championed critical questioning, while Aristotle's *Rhetoric* formalised persuasive argumentation. Medieval scholastic disputation refined logical reasoning, and Renaissance thinkers revived classical rhetoric. By the 18th century, debating societies flourished, promoting free speech and democratic ideals. Today, debate remains vital for fostering reasoned discourse, countering polarisation, and upholding democratic principles.

Benefits in the Classroom

Debate enhances critical thinking, communication, and collaboration — key 21st-century skills. Research shows it improves literacy, engagement, and academic performance, particularly for disadvantaged students. Studies from Finland, the US, and the UK demonstrate that structured debate deepens subject knowledge, sharpens reasoning, and builds confidence. It also strengthens language proficiency, with debaters outperforming peers in reading and writing. Beyond academics, debate cultivates civic awareness, encouraging students to engage with diverse perspectives and participate in democratic life.

The Education Policy Gap

Despite Australia's national education goals — promoting excellence, equity, and active citizenship — student achievement in literacy, numeracy, and civics has declined. NAPLAN and PISA results reveal stagnating proficiency, with many students failing to meet basic standards. Civics education is particularly weak, with only 38% of Year 10 students reaching proficiency in NAP-CC tests. Given debate's proven benefits, integrating it into civics and broader curricula could address these gaps, equipping students with the skills to engage in informed democratic discourse.

The Place of Debate in the Australian Curriculum

The Australian Curriculum for Foundation to Year 10 comprises eight learning areas, seven General Capabilities, and three Cross-Curriculum Priorities. While debate is occasionally referenced across these dimensions, most mentions are optional, leaving its inclusion dependent on individual teacher interest.

English

Debate appears sporadically in the English curriculum, though its implementation remains discretionary. (Appendix 1 of the full report outlines additional references to debate in other subject areas.)

Civics and Citizenship

Civics and Citizenship (Years 7-10) aims to develop active and informed citizens through skills like communication. While debates are suggested as a teaching approach, there is no explicit connection made between debate and democratic principles. This lack of emphasis may contribute to waning support for democracy among younger Australians, with only 65% of those aged 18-44 preferring it over other systems, compared to 79% of over-45s.

By contrast, Singapore's education system integrates Character and Citizenship Education (CCE) as a core priority, fostering shared values and civic engagement.

General Capabilities and Cross-Curriculum Priorities

Among the seven General Capabilities, **Critical and Creative Thinking** — structured around inquiry, analysis, and reflection — provides a natural fit for debate. The three Cross-Curriculum Priorities (Indigenous histories, Asia-Australia engagement, and Sustainability) also offer opportunities for debating skills development.

Senior Secondary

In Years 11-12, debate is referenced in subjects like English, Geography, and Humanities, though requirements vary. While some subjects encourage debating, others merely explore its role in academic discourse without mandating student participation.

Debating as an Extra-Curricular Activity

Debate is often treated as an optional extra-curricular activity, creating inequities where only well-resourced schools can offer it. Around 30,000 Australian students participate in debating competitions annually, benefiting from improved public speaking, argumentation, and critical thinking. Organisations like the **English-Speaking Union** advocate for greater emphasis on oracy in education.

Conclusion and Recommendations

Given Australia's declining literacy and civics outcomes, integrating debate into the curriculum could enhance English proficiency, critical thinking, and democratic engagement. To achieve this, policymakers should:

1. **Develop a national framework** aligning debate with curriculum goals, evidence-based pedagogy, and democratic values.
2. **Prioritise debate in literacy strategies** to strengthen language and reasoning skills.
3. **Ensure teacher training** includes debate as a core pedagogical tool.
4. **Expand professional development** in collaboration with debating organisations.

By embedding debate systematically, Australia can better equip students with the skills needed for academic success and active citizenship.

> This is a summary of a Centre for Independent Studies research paper. The full paper can be found at https://www.cis.org.au/publication/fortifying-a-healthy-democracy-why-young-australians-must-learn-the-art-of-debate/

30

The Way Forward for the Australian Curriculum

Fiona Mueller

These difficult times should stimulate deep thinking about nationhood and how young Australians can really learn to be "reflective, active and informed decision-makers, [who] will be well placed to contribute to an evolving and healthy democracy that fosters the wellbeing of Australia as a democratic nation" — as the curriculum goals state.

An effective national curriculum is the most powerful vehicle for reinforcing the foundations of citizenship. That requires at least some agreement on what Australia is, how it came to be, and what it wants to be, with clear connections made between its national heritage and its national goals.

Part of that means learning to debate freely and intelligently on the basis of extensive knowledge. Students, teachers, parents, employers and all other interested stakeholders deserve a clear line of sight between the official aims of education and their own efforts and aspirations.

But the most critical component needed to guide the Australian Curriculum review – an intellectually sophisticated, transparent and practical framework – is nowhere to be found. A framework of that quality — just as necessary in a successful business or other enterprise – would establish the basis for decisions about what to keep, modify or throw out, and identify the precise strategies and resources needed to get the job done.

Focusing the curriculum on Australia's cultural and intellectual heritage would provide a solid, cohesive foundation for all subject areas and create logical spaces for teachers to weave in material appropriate to local students and communities.

As with the very different approaches to school closures during the pandemic, the status of civics and citizenship within the Australian Curriculum highlights the weaknesses and inconsistencies of education in this country.

The 2019 Alice Springs (Mparntwe) Declaration is at the top of the list of documents that guided the previous curriculum review. The declaration is clear about the need to "teach young Australians the value of our nation's rich history", and expresses this in the context of "welcoming and valuing the local, regional and national cultural knowledge and the experiences of Aboriginal and Torres Strait Islander peoples".

In contrast, despite stated aims of instilling "an understanding of Australia's system of government, its histories, religions and culture", the declaration never formally acknowledges the richness and complexity of thousands of years of Western civilisation.

If students are to develop a sense of belonging and motivation to contribute to the national wellbeing, they need consistent and connected exposure to great ideas, events and people from history. For example, Australia's commitment to the principle of justice lends itself to a streamlined approach to the study of languages and literature, history, economics, the arts, science (especially medical) and other subjects.

According to its rationale, the Australian Curriculum "contributes to improving the quality, equity and transparency of Australia's education system". However, there was no public consultation prior to publishing the terms of reference, and the schedule contains only a brief window of opportunity for comment on the proposals for change.

This only compounds the essential problem: that too few see education as an issue of significance — and even fewer seem keen to ensure that it helps to build a nation.

This opinion piece was originally published by the *Canberra Times*.

SECTION 5

Higher Education
– Universities, Students, and Standards

For decades, Australia's universities were admired as engines of innovation, social mobility, and civic formation. Now, they seem increasingly adrift — pulled by political pressures, swamped by regulation, and entangled in a business model that incentivises mass enrolment over academic excellence. This section examines how higher education has changed, why it matters, and what might be done to restore its purpose.

In *Why Stop at Ending HECS-HELP for Failing Students?* Steven Schwartz addresses the staggering accumulation of student debt — now exceeding $70 billion — and the moral hazard it represents. He supports the government's move to restrict loans for students who fail more than half their subjects, but argues the reform doesn't go far enough. Until universities share in the cost of unpaid student loans, they have every incentive to admit marginal students and little motivation to ensure teaching quality. Making universities partly liable for unpaid loans, Schwartz contends, would align their interests with both student success and taxpayer value.

This call for institutional accountability is echoed in *Make Universities Pay for Picking Poorly Prepared Students.* There, Schwartz highlights the LANTITE test for aspiring teachers, which reveals how teacher training programs routinely admit students lacking basic literacy and numeracy. Again, the issue is not access, but misaligned incentives—universities benefit financially from enrolments, whether students thrive or fail.

Admission standards are also the focus of Rob Joseph. In *ATAR's Rising*

Relevance: Admission Standards and Completion Rates, he describes the relationship between lower admission standards and course completion.

Andrew Norton picks up another aspect of government policy in *Job-Ready Graduates 2.0*, a critique of the government's latest effort to match degrees to workforce needs via centralised planning. The irony is rich: a government attempting to engineer graduate pipelines even as labour markets shift more rapidly than policy can respond. Central control, Norton suggests, risks locking universities into irrelevance.

A related problem, Schwartz argues in *Freedom, Not More Red Tape, Will Save Universities*, is bureaucratic overreach. Universities are increasingly shackled by regulatory demands, with more agencies, committees, and compliance officers than ever before. The solution isn't tighter controls, but restored autonomy paired with real, performance-based accountability.

Academic freedom is a related casualty. In *Five Ways Unis Can Advance Free Expression* and *Campuses Should Not Be Safe Spaces to Breed Intolerance*, Schwartz documents how universities have surrendered their historic role as forums for vigorous debate. Safe spaces, trigger warnings, and cancellation campaigns have replaced critical inquiry with ideological conformity. He offers a practical roadmap to re-establish a culture of free and fearless discussion.

Several essays widen the lens. In *A Shorter Path to Teaching,* Rob Joseph explores alternative teacher preparation pathways that preserve standards while reducing unnecessary barriers. In *Degree Inflation,* Schwartz scrutinises the value of the university credential itself, asking why more degrees haven't delivered more economic or civic return. Schwartz's *Déjà Vu in Australian Higher Education* reminds us that these debates are not new — only more urgent.

Finally, in *Eliminating the F Word — Failure,* Schwartz explores the cultural shift away from academic standards altogether. When universities treat all students as customers and all outcomes as equally valid, the idea of failure becomes politically incorrect, even as disengagement and underperformance rise.

Together, these essays reveal a system where good intentions — equity, access, growth — have produced perverse results: ballooning debt, eroded standards, bureaucratic sprawl, and intellectual stagnation. The reforms proposed here are not nostalgic or punitive. They are rooted in a belief that higher education still matters — so long as it remembers what it is for.

31

Hold Universities Accountable for Admission Decisions

Steven Schwartz

Some students have accumulated hundreds of thousands of dollars in student debt without obtaining a qualification. In response, the government has proposed restricting access to government-subsidised student loans. Unless there is a compelling explanation, students who fail half their first eight subjects will be unable to access loans. This proposal represents a vital reform of the student loan system, but more needs to be done.

The philosophy underlying student loans is sound. Income-contingent student loans are an efficient, fair, and attractive way to for students to invest in their education. Unlike credit card or mortgage loans, it is impossible to default on an income-contingent loan because repayments are matched to a graduate's income. Graduates who are out of work, take time off to raise children or never reach the earning threshold, have no obligation to make payments. Because tuition fees need to be paid upfront, income-contingent loans make access to higher education a matter of brains, not bankbooks; but they come at a cost. If graduates never earn enough money to repay their loans, taxpayers absorb the loss.

The total amount owed by students is approaching $70 billion, more than double Australia's national credit card debt. Last year, the government estimated that 16% of student debt would never be repaid. The amount is likely to be much higher in an economy wracked by COVID-19. Taxpayers, if there are any left, will have to cover the cost.

Although they serve a worthy social purpose, income-contingent loans also provide many opportunities for what economists call 'moral hazard'. (Moral hazard is a fancy term for taking risks and sticking someone else with the consequences.) For example, the loan system encourages students to borrow more than they would if loan repayments were not income-contingent. (Around 6% of graduates owe $100,000 or more.) Students take on high levels of debt because the government is taking most of the risk. If graduates benefit from their education and reach the income repayment threshold, they repay their loans. If they never reach the income threshold, they are not required to make repayments, and the government absorbs the loss.

Imagine offering loans to stock market speculators on similar terms. If they make a killing, they repay their loan and keep the profit. If their investments collapse, the taxpayer makes good their losses. Who wouldn't accept such a deal?

Moral hazard also applies to universities. Because they receive their fees upfront from the government — actually from taxpayers –and are not responsible for collecting loan repayments, they may be tempted to admit academically marginal students. After all, it is not the universities, but the taxpayers that have to cope with any losses.

Limiting loans for failing students is one way to make universities accept part of the repayment risk. But it is not only failing students who do not repay their loans. The government should also consider making universities partly responsible for the unpaid loans of students who manage to graduate but never earn enough to repay their loans.

Universities would be more careful about the students they admit, their course offerings, and the effectiveness of their teaching if they had skin in the loan-repayment game.

The income-contingent loan system insulates universities and students from losses. At the same time, the government (on behalf of the shrinking number of taxpayers) bears most of the risk. Reducing failing students' access to loans is an excellent first step. Still, the system could be improved further by moving more of the risk to universities.

This opinion piece was originally published by *The Spectator*.

32

Make Universities Pay for Picking Poorly Prepared Students

Steven Schwartz

Universities have drastically dropped their entry requirements for teaching degrees, resulting in a hit on the taxpayer when many students inevitably fail to graduate.

Take Jayden (not his real name). He barely squeaked through school. His Australian Tertiary Admission Rank placed him in the bottom half of school-leavers. Nevertheless, he was admitted to a university Bachelor of Education program to train to be a teacher. Compared with school, Jayden found university undemanding. Neither his idiosyncratic spelling nor his uncertain grammar affected his marks. He seemed destined for a teaching career until he hit a snag.

Like all prospective teachers, he was required to undertake the Literacy and Numeracy Test for Initial Teacher Education Students, an examination designed to ensure that graduates have the fundamental cognitive skills needed to be effective teachers.

It is hardly difficult. Jayden's university advises students to prepare for it by studying the National Assessment Program — Literacy and Numeracy tests used to assess school students. Alas, this did not suffice. Jayden failed both the literacy and numeracy parts of the LANTITE. He can retake the test, but if 12 years at school and several more at a university were unable to prepare him, cramming a few old NAPLAN tests is unlikely to make a difference.

Jayden isn't unique. Last year, more than 1500 candidates failed the numeracy or the literacy component of the LANTITE. By keeping them from entering the classroom, the LANTITE ensures a minimum level of teacher quality. However, this assurance comes at a high cost. Candidates do not sit the examination until after a year or more of university study, which means they already have incurred student fee loans. Those who fail the LANTITE cannot teach, and their studies do not equip them for any other job, so they are unable to repay their loans. Taxpayers must pick up the tab.

A less expensive way to improve the capabilities of future teachers is to raise the ATAR required for admission to teacher education courses. This is the approach favoured by opposition education spokeswoman Tanya Plibersek. Under her plan, poorly prepared students would not be lumbered with student loans because they would not be admitted to university.

Improving teacher quality by increasing the ATARs seems straightforward, but it also has problems. As Universities Australia, the peak body for Australian universities, was quick to point out, the ATAR is just one of several indicators that universities use to select students. If the government required higher ATARs for entry to education courses, universities could swap to other measures. In any event, mandating entry standards — telling universities whom they can admit — is a dangerous precedent for government. To avoid political interference, universities must be free to decide which students to accept.

Instead of focusing on ATARs, the government could limit the number of students studying education. Capping the number of teacher education students would force students to compete for places, which would drive up entry standards.

The difficulty with this approach is knowing where to set the cap. The government's record on predicting workforce needs is dismal. (In the 1990s, the government predicted a glut of doctors. A few years later, it predicted a shortage.) Setting the cap too low could result in teacher shortages.

If teacher education places were capped, universities might direct students with low ATARs into other programs, where similar quality issues will arise. Australia wants more than just high-quality teachers; the country deserves competent graduates in all fields.

Another way to encourage universities to improve the quality of graduates is to focus on the reason they are willing to accept poorly prepared students in the first place: money. Students pay tuition fees to the university. These fees are funded by government-backed loans. Universities retain students' fees regardless of whether graduates ever repay their loans. Because universities bear none of the repayment risk, they are incentivised to accept poorly prepared students. If these students fail to repay their loans, it is the taxpayers — not the universities — who are stuck with the losses.

Formal examinations, government-mandated ATAR scores and capped places may increase teacher quality, but they all have significant drawbacks. The best way for government to improve the quality of graduates is to require universities to share the repayment risk associated with student loans. Specifically, each university should be made liable for a portion of its students' unpaid loans.

Given that student debt is already larger than Australia's total credit card debt, assigning even a small share to universities would have a powerful effect on their behaviour. To reduce their risk, universities would have to be careful about whom they admit, the courses they offer and the skills they impart.

Students, employers and the economy would all benefit. Graduate quality would increase, and the growing mountain of student debt would finally begin to shrink.

This opinion piece was originally published by *The Australian*.

33

ATAR's Rising Relevance: Admission Standards and Completion Rates

Rob Joseph

Executive Summary

For more than a decade there has been an ongoing debate around ATAR's suitability and future, and in particular, its role in university admissions criteria. This debate is especially relevant today when more school leavers are failing to finish their university degree on-time (completion) or are dropping out of university entirely (attrition).

This paper looks at past research and recent data on ATAR with respect to university admissions, completions, and attrition, with a particular focus on the growing category of students admitted on a non-ATAR basis.

ATAR remains the dominant pathway to university for school leavers. Recent estimates show almost three-in-four school leavers use ATAR to gain university entry; 60% use solely ATAR, and 14% use ATAR in conjunction with other criteria. The share admitted on a non-ATAR basis has grown from 15% in 2016 to at least 25% today.

ATAR is significantly associated with completions and attrition; with each ascending ATAR band, completions rise and attrition fall. Low ATAR students (with scores of 0-60) drop out at rates about three times that of high ATAR students (80-100).

Non-ATAR based admissions are almost twice as likely as ATAR-based admissions to drop out of university in their first year. Additionally, completion rates are falling faster for non-ATAR based admissions than any other ATAR band, declining by 4.9 percentage points over the decade, over twice the drop for all school leavers.

Despite rhetoric around non-ATAR pathways being 'fairer' or more 'equitable', in practice universities appear to be using this method as an opaque way to admit low-ATAR students, without commensurate increases in support needed to complete their degrees.

The Australian Government could help address these problems in admissions, completions, and attrition for school leavers by reforming transparency and financial incentives for universities.

On transparency, the government should require universities to record any ATARs of school leavers admitted on a non-ATAR basis. Additionally, admission reporting standards for universities should be shifted from a voluntary to a mandatory basis, given the longstanding problem of many universities not complying with reporting guidelines.

On financial incentives, when school leavers drop out of higher education, universities should be required to pay a share of the government's contribution to those students' tuition costs. This would correct the distorted financial incentives for universities – to enrol as many students as possible and teach them as cheaply as possible – and encourage them to invest in making their admissions process more rigorous and to improve support for students at risk of attrition.

On early intervention measures, universities should be required to have in place procedures that identify students at risk of attrition, then provide either remedial support well in advance or else remind them of the option to drop out earlier before incurring financial debt.

Even small improvements in completion rates could benefit substantial numbers of young people. Using the most recent school leaver estimates from Course Seeker (2018 to 2022), if completion rates for students admitted on a non-ATAR basis could be increased to that of those admitted on an ATAR basis, an extra 3,800 students would finish their degrees each year.

Introduction

The Australian Tertiary Admission Rank (ATAR) is a percentile ranking used to assess a student's academic performance relative to their peers and is commonly used for university admissions. Despite being a standardised and rigorous tool, ATAR has come under increasing criticism, with detractors labelling it outdated, narrow, and stressful, and arguing it fails to account for broader skills, life experience, and disadvantage. Various educational reviews have called for the reduction or elimination of ATAR, proposing alternatives like Learner Profiles that provide a more holistic view of student capabilities. However, such alternatives may unintentionally favour more privileged students. Although there is considerable debate around the value of ATAR, claims about its declining use and predictive value are rarely backed by recent data. This paper aims to clarify ATAR's current role in university admissions and its relationship to student outcomes like completion and attrition.

Background on Australian Universities

Australia has 43 universities, including 38 public and five private institutions, with over 1.1 million domestic and 400,000 international enrolments. Universities Australia represents 39 of these institutions, while sub-groups like the Group of Eight focus on specific interests, such as research intensity.

Funding

Domestic undergraduate students generally occupy Commonwealth Supported Places (CSPs), with costs subsidised by the government through the Commonwealth Grant Scheme (CGS) and the remainder paid by students, often via income-contingent loans like HECS-HELP. In 2020, CSP funding was 58% government and 42% student contribution. Australia spends 1.92% of its GDP on tertiary education, with two-thirds being private expenditure, including student loans. Recent funding reforms include discipline-based cost adjustments (2021), restrictions on financial support for students failing more than half their subjects (2022), and a performance-based funding scheme starting in 2024, measuring outcomes like graduate employment and student success.

Admission Pathways

Undergraduate students in Australia gain entry through various pathways, with at least 43% being recent school leavers. They apply either directly to universities or through tertiary admission centres (TACs), which also calculate ATARs. The Course Seeker site categorises admissions into three types: based solely on ATAR, based on ATAR plus additional criteria, and based entirely on other criteria. Universities may also apply adjustment factors—such as for equity, subject choice, or location—that modify an applicant's selection rank. Alternative pathways exist for students who do not meet standard entry requirements, including preparatory courses, mature-aged entry, or transferring after one year of study in another course.

The 'Demand-Driven System'

Between 2010 and 2017, the demand-driven system allowed unlimited government-funded university places, aiming to boost participation and access for underrepresented groups. This led to more low-ATAR students entering university and succeeded in raising enrolment and equity levels. However, concerns emerged around student preparedness and academic performance, as highlighted by the Productivity Commission in 2019. Despite the system ending, enrolments remain high, and the government continues to pursue similar access goals, such as the recent announcement of 20,000 new places.

Early Offers

Universities increasingly use early offer schemes, where students receive conditional or unconditional offers before finishing Year 12, based on academic and non-academic criteria. Although early offers can reduce exam stress, they have raised concerns about diminishing student motivation and undermining ATAR's role. In 2023, approximately 39,000 early offers were made in NSW and ACT. These schemes are now under review, with expectations of future limits or adjustments to their use.

Completions And Attrition For School Leavers At University

Student non-completion and attrition rates are rising, especially among school leavers. Around 30% do not complete their degrees within six years, and nearly 20% drop out entirely. This equates to over 34,000 students annually starting degrees they will not finish on time, including more than 20,000 who will drop out. This has serious financial implications for students and the public, and raises concerns about university admission and support practices. While some dropout is unavoidable, persistent trends suggest systemic issues. Universities share responsibility for enrolling students capable of succeeding and for offering adequate academic support. The Higher Education Standards Framework mandates that institutions demonstrate responsible admissions and effective student support systems. As ATAR is still the most commonly used admission tool, its role is central to addressing these challenges.

ATAR And University Admission Pathways for School Leavers

Between 2018 and 2022, nearly 75% of school leavers used ATAR for university admissions, a slight decline from 85% in 2016. Around 60% were admitted solely on ATAR, and another 14% used ATAR alongside other criteria. In 2020, school leavers comprised about 43% of new domestic Bachelor students, with the rest coming from VET, work, or other tertiary study. Non-ATAR admissions vary by university, reaching 100% at the University of Divinity and 87% at Notre Dame. At Macquarie University, alternative criteria such as the Academic Entry Program are used. Over the past decade, universities have relaxed admission standards, with offer rates rising across all ATAR bands, especially for those below 60.

ATAR and Completion Rates for School Leavers at University

Government data shows ATAR strongly predicts university completion and attrition rates. Six-year completion rates drop from 87% for ATARs of 95–100 to 46% for those between 30–49, while attrition rises from 4% to 39% across the same range. University-level variation is substantial: completion is lowest at the University of Southern Queensland (43%) and highest at the University of Melbourne (90%).

Completion Rates for School Leavers Admitted on A Non-ATAR Basis

Around 25% of school leavers—nearly 27,000 annually—are admitted without an ATAR, a share that has grown over time. This group has poorer outcomes, with only 59% completing within six years and 27% dropping out. Their outcomes resemble students with ATARs of 60–69, but first-year attrition is nearly double that of ATAR-based peers. Completion rates for non-ATAR students have fallen more sharply than any other group, with about 1,300 more students each year failing to complete compared to 2005. Although alternative admissions are often promoted as fairer, in practice they have led to worse outcomes for many. Nonetheless, there are standout institutions, such as Notre Dame, where non-ATAR admissions achieve a 72% completion rate. If completion rates for these students matched their ATAR-based peers, an additional 3,800 students would graduate annually.

Equity Considerations and Risk-Based Approaches to Admissions

Research confirms standardised academic performance is a strong predictor of university success. However, institutional factors—such as quality teaching and financial support—also influence outcomes. Overly rigid academic requirements may unfairly exclude capable students, and admissions staff often lack full information to make optimal decisions. A nuanced, risk-based approach is needed, especially for those with low or no ATARs. These students still have a 50% chance of completing, and better screening—using subject-specific marks and broader profiles—could help identify those most likely to succeed. Universities can also assist by highlighting critical deadlines like census dates and using early warning systems. Rigorous admissions need not conflict with equity if data and support mechanisms are properly utilised.

Conclusion

Reports of ATAR's decline are unfounded. It remains the primary pathway for school leavers and is strongly linked to student success. Given declining completion rates, ATAR's relevance is growing. Non-ATAR pathways have generally produced worse outcomes, often without genuine consideration of student preparedness. ATAR should not be the only criterion, but where available, it should always be part of the assessment. Many students who drop out might have succeeded with better preparation or support—or may have been better served by vocational or employment pathways. Universities have a responsibility not only to widen access but to ensure students can complete their studies. Falling completion rates demand accountability, and ATAR remains essential in diagnosing and addressing these issues.

Recommendations

While questions remain about whether universities should have full autonomy over admissions, there are practical steps the Australian Government can take to improve completion and attrition outcomes without removing that autonomy.

1. Improving Transparency

The government can enhance transparency by mandating that universities report the ATAR of all school leavers, even those admitted on non-ATAR bases, if an ATAR exists. This would expose whether non-ATAR pathways are genuinely holistic or being used to admit students unlikely to complete their degrees. A proposed loophole that exempts universities from reporting if no places are offered on the basis of ATAR should be rejected.

Compliance and standardisation of reporting also need improvement. The Course Seeker website often lacks current student profile data, and over a dozen universities have not published updated information. Many are years behind on their transparency commitments. Making this reporting mandatory and prioritised by government would address persistent issues highlighted by TEQSA.

Additionally, researchers need better access to relevant data. Too many requests are denied, and data are often only available in aggregated or limited form. Policies should aim to reveal university performance, not obscure it.

2. Improving Financial Incentives

Current funding arrangements reward universities for enrolment volume, with no penalty if students drop out or fail to complete. The new performance-based funding model set for 2024 includes attrition rates, but the impact will be minimal—potentially reducing a university's funding by just 0.6% for poor performance.

A more meaningful approach would see universities bear some financial cost when school leavers fail to complete their degrees. This would encourage more rigorous admissions processes and greater investment in student support. Given school leavers' limited experience in financial and career decisions, universities have a duty of care that should be reflected in the financial risk they assume.

3. Improving Early Intervention

There are also ways to reduce attrition through earlier engagement. Students should be prompted via text messages before census dates, and universities should proactively check for disengagement. Opt-in confirmations of enrolment before fees are incurred could also reduce passive attrition.

Students choosing part-time or off-campus modes should be warned of the higher risks of dropping out. Universities should further expand the use of predictive analytics to monitor student engagement and anticipate drop-out risk. These models, already in use in some institutions, can provide early warnings based on patterns such as access to learning materials and changes in study behaviour.

If universities continue to admit higher-risk students, they must match this with more robust strategies either to prevent attrition or to ensure students exit before incurring financial harm.

> This is a summary of a Centre for Independent Studies research paper. The full paper can be found at https://www.cis.org.au/publication/atars-rising-relevance-admission-standards-and-completion-rates/

34

Job-Ready Graduates 2.0: The Universities Accord and Centralised Control of Universities and Courses

Andrew Norton

Australia's graduate labour market does not always seem to function well. Graduates with degrees in some fields struggle to find suitable work, while employers cannot fill vacancies in occupations that rely on graduates.

The former Morrison and current Albanese governments share an interest in these problems, but with contrasting policy responses.

To steer student choices, the Morrison government's Job-ready Graduates policy discounted student charges for preferred courses and doubled them for courses deemed less 'job ready'. But it did not intervene in university supply decisions, instead giving universities more flexibility in moving public funding between courses. It was a demand-side intervention.

The Albanese government's Australian Universities Accord review aims to replace Job-ready Graduates with supply-side interventions, increasing or decreasing numbers of student places in different courses according to perceived needs.

The Universities Accord interim report is vague on important details. But its authors clearly want to replace current decentralised modes of decision-making, under which universities and students coordinate the allocation of student places to courses, with a more centralised and bureaucratic system of control.

A new regulator, the Australian Tertiary Education Commission (TEC), would be responsible for increases or decreases in student places by courses at each university. It would be guided in these decisions by Jobs and Skills Australia, a government labour market analytics agency.

Detailed ATEC control of enrolments would overturn longstanding practices of allocating most public university funding in a flexible way. Historically, block grants are the most common funding method. In this system, universities decide which courses to fund within a capped overall amount. Under a less common system, demand driven funding, university decisions are not constrained by a funding cap.

However, no system of allocating funding to universities can abolish apparent mismatches between degrees and jobs. Not all university students enrol for employment reasons, and the options of those that do are constrained by their academic abilities and their interests. Few people will commit to a course or career that does not interest them.

The labour market can change more quickly than the flow of graduates from three-year degrees. The number of professional jobs in skills shortage has almost tripled since 2021. The 2010s graduate boom times predicted by a previous higher education review were instead the worst ever period for new graduates looking for work.

Perfect alignment between graduates and jobs is impossible, but we can design systems to adapt quickly to emerging employment opportunities and risks.

The centralised approach preferred by the Universities Accord interim report is unlikely to outperform the more flexible block grant or demand driven systems. Its decision making would be on a bureaucratic cycle, responding more slowly than universities observing changes in student applications. Bureaucratic systems could lock public funding into yesterday's labour market needs, causing stranded resources that cannot be used effectively.

Australia's one long-term experience of bureaucratic allocation of student places, for medical courses, is not encouraging. Australia relies on doctors from overseas and has many doctor job vacancies.

The Universities Accord final report should drop its plan for more university bureaucracy. Decentralised decision-making by universities and students is a lower-risk way of achieving its labour market goals.

Trends in Graduate Outcomes

Graduate employment rates have declined steadily over the past decade, with a growing mismatch between the number of graduates produced and the availability of relevant jobs. Data from the Department of Education reveals a sharp drop in graduate employment rates, particularly in professional fields such as law, business, and the humanities. While some sectors experience shortages of skilled workers, others face an oversupply of graduates competing for limited positions. Underemployment—where graduates take roles that do not require a degree—is also rising, indicating broader structural issues in aligning education with workforce demands.

Predicting Future Labour Market Needs

Accurately forecasting graduate labour market needs remains a complex challenge. Efforts by governments to direct student enrolments toward high-demand fields often fail due to long lead times in education and rapidly changing economic conditions. For example, policy shifts encouraging more students to pursue science, technology, engineering, and mathematics (STEM) degrees have led to surges in supply without corresponding increases in job opportunities. These mismatches suggest that rigid planning mechanisms may not be well-suited to the dynamic nature of the labour market.

Student Choice and Course Preferences

Student preferences play a critical role in shaping graduate outcomes, yet they are often overlooked in policy design. Student choices are constrained by their school results and their interests; few students will commit to courses and careers that they won't enjoy. While applications for vocationally-oriented courses tend to follow labour market trends, many students gravitate toward courses that interest them despite weak job prospects. Attempts to steer students away from oversubscribed disciplines through financial incentives have had limited success, highlighting the difficulty of influencing individual decision-making at scale.

Risk of Unused Public Resources

Centralised funding models risk inefficient use of public resources when student demand does not match allocated funding. For instance, government efforts to expand enrolments in specific priority areas have sometimes resulted in unfilled places due to low student interest. Conversely, high-demand courses often face capacity constraints, limiting access for qualified applicants. These imbalances demonstrate the limitations of top-down planning in a diverse and evolving higher education landscape.

Conclusion

All university funding systems face common constraints. Student interests and abilities limit which courses they will choose. Uncertain future labour market conditions make it hard to predict vacancies for graduates three or four years in the future. An ideal outcome for all graduates and all employers is not feasible. But within these constraints we can adopt better and worse policy options. Centralised university funding models struggle to predict and adapt to changing economic conditions. Centralised funding can lock resources into universities and courses for which there is insufficient demand. More adaptable models, such as the current flexible block grants or the previous demand driven funding system, do a better job of matching enrolments with real-world trends.

> This is a summary of a Centre for Independent Studies research paper. The full paper can be found at https://www.cis.org.au/publication/job-ready-graduates-2-0-the-universities-accord-and-centralised-control-of-universities-and-courses/

35

Freedom, Not More Red Tape, Will Save Universities

Steven Schwartz

Senator Tony Sheldon, Chair of the Senate's Education and Employment Committee, is seeking an inquiry into what he ominously calls a "spate" of governance issues at universities. His checklist is a mix of familiar grievances and new headline fodder: "wage theft" from casual workers, a pathetic reaction to campus antisemitism, extravagant spending on consultants, and concern over the composition, transparency, and accountability of university governing bodies. Vice chancellors' pay, often topping a million dollars, will also be scrutinised, along with the money they spend decorating their offices or throwing "parties".

All this unfolds against a backdrop of mounting challenges. Universities, once darlings of public trust, are now seeking community support while trying to fend off government restrictions on their lucrative international student markets. Domestic student enrolments are dropping, public confidence is eroding, and the sector is drowning in compliance burdens.

The government's response? More oversight, more watchdogs, more red tape. This is the Australian way, after all: if a problem exists, create a committee; if it persists, establish an agency; and if it thrives, bury it under so much red tape that no one can tell where the problem ends, and bureaucracy begins.

It's not as if problems don't exist. Casual workers were underpaid — although it was more likely a result of clunky payroll systems than sinister wage theft. Vice chancellors are paid handsomely, and a few may have made questionable choices about office décor. But the solution to these problems isn't to create endless agencies or commissions. What universities need isn't more bureaucracy; they need better internal governance.

Instead of representatives of interest groups (the current model), university governing bodies (councils or senates) should be composed of talented people who are properly prepared for their roles and who represent a wide array of perspectives. An informed Council is a university's best defence against 'groupthink' — the bureaucratic echo chamber where bad decisions are made quietly, by consensus.

But governance goes beyond good intentions and well-rounded resumes. University councils also need independence. Right now, they rely on university bureaucrats to feed them information — often carefully sanitised to avoid ruffling feathers. Councils must have dedicated staff who report directly to them, ensuring they are fully informed about all issues. Without an unbiased source of information, Councils risk becoming rubber-stamping bodies, nodding along to whatever the university administration presents.

The government's obsession with central control only makes things worse. In addition to the elephantine Tertiary Education Quality and Standards Agency, the Tertiary Education Commission is being exhumed after being buried for 40 years. This body (pun intended) is supposed to bring order to the sector, but in practice, it will lead to more uniformity, less flexibility, and a sprawling bureaucracy of its own. Add the newly announced student complaints agency, which is tailor-made to encourage grievances, and it's hard to see how universities will have time for anything other than filling out forms.

Even the government's newly appointed advisory body on vice chancellors' pay misses the mark. Yes, some salaries are eye-watering, but the solution isn't another layer of oversight — it's helping universities fix themselves. Councils must be empowered to govern effectively, with the training needed to steer institutions through turbulent times. A one-size-fits-all approach will only lead to mediocrity.

Friedrich Hayek famously warned against the "fatal conceit" of central planning — the idea that bureaucrats can manage complex systems better than the people directly involved. Universities are prime examples of this principle. They thrive on competition, innovation, and autonomy. Centralisation stifles all three.

Universities don't need more watchdogs, agencies, or commissions. They need councils that are strong, informed, and capable of making tough decisions. They need the freedom to compete and innovate, and, above all, universities need to stop being treated like wayward children in need of constant supervision.

The best way to govern a university is to let it govern itself and insist it does so properly. Educate council members, give them the support they require, hold them publicly accountable for outcomes and sack them and their vice chancellors when they fail. It's not a flashy strategy, and it won't win headlines, but it might just save our universities from drowning in red tape.

Universities are Australia's engines of innovation and social mobility. But they can't thrive if they're suffocated by bureaucracy or stripped of autonomy. The government's obsession with control will produce universities that are obedient but uninspired, compliant but uncompetitive. It's time to stop managing universities into mediocrity and start encouraging them to excel.

Freedom, not red tape, is what will save them.

> This opinion piece was originally published by the *Australian Financial Review*.

36

Five Ways Unis Can Advance Free Expression

Steven Schwartz

"If liberty means anything at all, it means the right to tell people what they do not want to hear," George Orwell wrote in *Animal Farm*.

At a 1943 symposium, University of Sydney professor of philosophy John Anderson spoke out against religion in the school curriculum. "Religious doctrines are a direct attack and assault on a child's common sense," he said. "If a child is forced to swallow doctrines of a religious nature, it will undermine his understanding of things in general".

The learned members of the NSW Legislative Assembly condemned Anderson's comments for undermining "the principles of the Constitution of the Christian state". Not one member of the assembly spoke in Anderson's support. The Legislative Council (parliament's other house) passed its own motion asking the governing body of Sydney University to "define the limits" universities should place on the discussion of controversial matters. The world still awaits its response.

Anderson was unrepentant. His call for campus speakers to be "as blasphemous, obscene and seditious as they like" was strongly supported by students, sympathetic colleagues and a few university leaders.

Fast-forward to the present. The right to speak on campus remains as contentious as ever but the protagonists have reversed roles. Politicians now lament campus censorship while students — and even academics — are becoming increasingly intolerant. Convinced of their own fragility, today's students believe exposure to challenging ideas can be harmful, even traumatic. Students demand to be "protected" from controversial speakers.

A poll of 3000 students in the US conducted by the Knight Foundation last year found 37 per cent believed it was acceptable to shout down speakers and 10 per cent thought using violence against speakers was sometimes acceptable. The Brookings Institution reports even larger numbers: 50 per cent of university students consider it acceptable to disrupt speakers by shouting, and 19 per cent condone the use of violence to silence those whose views they find objectionable.

One victim of student intolerance is sex therapist and columnist Bettina Arndt. Her heresy is to disagree with the conclusions of a report produced by the Australian Human Rights Commission, which claimed that 21 per cent of Australian university students were "sexually harassed" in a university setting.

Arndt pointed out that the commission's definition of harassment included unwanted compliments, leering, staring and bad jokes. The number of respondents who reported being assaulted was 1.6 per cent (and some of those incidents took place on public transport, not at the university). The incidence of sexual assault on campus is lower than the rate of sexual assault in the general community.

Students at Melbourne's La Trobe University invited Arndt to speak. At first, university administrators refused permission, claiming Arndt's views did not "align with the values of the university and its campaign ... against sexual violence on campus". It seems that La Trobe has an "official position" on sexual assault. As a consequence, the university would rather have students, and the public, believe its campus was unsafe than let Arndt speak. La Trobe relented when Arndt took her story to the press, but no one heard her speak. Protesters silenced her by shouting her down. Her next talk, at Sydney University, similarly was shouted down and required mobilising police to protect her and the audience from aggressive protesters.

In the 1940s, Anderson urged his students to fight hard for free speech "without restrictions". Today's student activists are intent on achieving the exact opposite.

Expressing alarm at the censorious environment on our campuses, Human

Rights Commissioner Ed Santow is encouraging universities to develop codes of conduct that protect robust debate.

Federal Education Minister Dan Tehan agrees, expressing support for the University of Chicago statement on principles of free expression, which commits universities to unfettered "debate and deliberation" even when "the ideas put forth are thought by some or even by most members of the university community to be offensive, unwise, immoral or wrongheaded". The statement also forbids anyone from interfering with the freedom of others to "express views they reject or even loathe". (That is, no shouting down speakers.) The Chicago statement has been adopted by dozens of American universities, but none in Australia.

Echoing Orwell, former High Court chief justice Robert French said this week that "offensive or hurtful" speech was the price we paid for liberty. He says universities erode their public standing and perhaps even face legislative intervention if they fail to defend free speech. French's prediction is not just hypothetical. The US states of Arizona and North Carolina already have legislated speech codes for their universities and so has the University of Wisconsin board of regents.

Australian universities would avoid the erosion of their public standing and advance liberty by adopting five rules.

- Affirm the value of free speech.
- Forbid administrators from disinviting speakers.
- Discipline students or staff who try to silence speakers.
- Remain institutionally neutral on matters of public policy.
- Levy security charges on all speakers, not just those on one side of an issue.

It is fitting to end where we began. After being condemned by parliament, Anderson addressed students. His words are worth repeating: "There is no absolute right of free speech. It exists only so far as people are prepared to maintain it and fight for it".

Universities owe it to the public to join the fray.

This opinion piece was originally published by *The Australian*.

37

Campuses Shouldn't be Safe Spaces to Breed Intolerance

Steven Schwartz

Once upon a time, Australian universities served a higher purpose: preparing students not just for careers, but for citizenship in a diverse, pluralistic society. At their best, they were melting pots—places where young people encountered others from different backgrounds, learned to navigate differences, and emerged more capable of engaging with the world beyond campus. Today, however, a curious trend has taken hold: the re-segregation of student housing, common areas, and even graduation ceremonies—this time along lines of race, religion, and sex. Universities insist this is progress. In truth, it is a step backward, a retreat from the ideals they once championed.

I grew up in the United States during an era when racial segregation was the law. Despite living in a city with a large Black population, I rarely encountered Black individuals. Schools, theatres, and sports facilities were divided by race, entrenching ignorance, prejudice, and mutual suspicion. The civil rights movement changed that. It was not an easy process—court-ordered busing, for instance, faced bitter resistance from both Black and white parents—but integration gradually dismantled the legal and psychological barriers that had kept people apart. Over time, diversity ceased to be an abstract ideal. Black mayors, Black police commissioners, even a Black president became part of the fabric of society.

Yet, in a strange and troubling twist, Australian universities are now actively undoing this painful progress. Racially exclusive computer labs sparked controversy when non-Aboriginal students at the Queensland University of Technology attempted to use them. The University of

Technology Sydney is building a National First Nations College. James Cook University is just one of at least seven in Australia that either hold separate graduation ceremonies for Indigenous students or allow them to wear sashes differentiating themselves from the rest of the graduating cohort.

Universities justify these initiatives as necessary for "support" and "inclusion". The irony is striking: the very structures once used to exclude minorities are being reintroduced, this time under the banner of social justice. But segregation—even well-intentioned segregation—does not empower. It isolates. It tells students they are too fragile to coexist with those unlike them. Worse, it deprives them of the very skills a diverse society requires: the ability to engage, to debate, and to find common ground.

Proponents argue that separate spaces allow historically marginalised groups to find solace and solidarity without the fear of bias. But universities exist to prepare students for the real world. And in the real world, people must live, work, and collaborate across lines of race, religion, and gender. If students are trained to retreat into self-imposed enclaves at the first sign of discomfort, how will they develop the resilience and adaptability that higher education is meant to foster?

This is not just a theoretical concern. Even voluntary segregation deepens divisions. It fosters an us-versus-them mentality, fuels stereotypes, and reinforces misunderstandings.

Historically, segregation was justified using arguments eerily similar to those heard today: different groups have unique needs, intermingling is risky, separation provides safety. The motivations may have changed, but the result is all too familiar: a fractured society where people increasingly see themselves as members of rigid identity groups rather than citizens of a shared community.

A common response is that modern segregation is optional, unlike its historical predecessors. But self-segregation still carries consequences. It normalises the idea that people should be sorted and separated by identity rather than encouraged to engage with one another. Worse, it reflects a broader cultural shift toward avoiding ideological and cultural differences instead of confronting them—a trend already reinforced by social media echo chambers and political polarisation.

This dilemma recently hit home at Macquarie University, where I once served as Vice-Chancellor. In response to rising campus antisemitism, administrators designated a "safe room" for Jewish students. The impulse was well-meant and understandable—students should not fear for their safety on campus—but it raised a deeper question: is the solution to hostility separation? Or should universities ensure that every student feels safe everywhere on campus? A university that cannot protect its students risks legitimising segregation as a permanent feature rather than addressing the root problem: intolerance.

Universities should resist the impulse to fragment their communities. There is nothing wrong with students forming friendships around shared experiences. Affinity groups and support networks have their place. But institutionalising separation—especially in the very spaces where students study, socialise, and interact—sends the wrong message. It tells students that difference is a problem to be managed through exclusion rather than engagement.

The modern university faces many challenges, but few are as urgent as the question of whether it will remain a place of integration or slide further into self-imposed division. A pluralistic society requires citizens who can engage across differences, not just coexist in parallel worlds.

If universities do not model this, who will?

> This opinion piece was originally published by *The Australian*.

38

Degree Inflation: Undermining The Value of Higher Education

Steven Schwartz

While universities continue expanding degree offerings, the economic value of these credentials is diminishing - a phenomenon this paper terms "degree inflation". We examine this trend's causes and consequences across five sections: documenting higher education's explosive growth, analysing its impact on graduates and non-graduates, assessing effects on national productivity, identifying growth drivers, and proposing policy solutions to make higher education more valuable and equitable.

Executive Summary

The past 20 years have seen explosive growth in universities. At the same time, vocational education and training (VET) faced a tsunami of financial challenges and poorly-implemented policies. As a result, VET is now stigmatised as a second-class education option, and employers demand university credentials for jobs that formerly did not require them. This credential inflation severely disadvantages those who have the ability and experience to perform a job but, for one reason or another, were unable to study at a university. Instead of increasing social mobility, the vast growth in degrees has had precisely the opposite effect.

As the number of graduates increased, the economic value of their degrees withered. Twenty per cent, or more, of today's university students, would have been better off financially by skipping university and going straight from school to work. The same is true for the thousands of students who drop out of university each year.

Yet, universities continue to churn out more degrees, each worth less than the previous one. They justify their behaviour with fatuous 'economic impact' studies designed to claim that universities are engines of economic growth. Even a cursory look at these studies reveals a shaky foundation of assumptions, assertions, and guesses. Because they ignore opportunity costs, economic impact studies are of no value in helping politicians decide where to focus government spending.

As degrees proliferate, many graduates find themselves working in fields other than the ones they studied at university. Universities claim their degrees remain relevant because they endow graduates with higher-order cognitive skills applicable to any job. They offer no objective evidence for this claim.

An end to degree inflation would bring many social and economic benefits. Employers would have access to a larger and more diverse pool of potential employees whose experience and skills render them equally — or even better — qualified than applicants with degrees. The value of further education, trade schools, military training, and on-the-job apprenticeships would be enhanced, as would life-long learning. Young people who aspire to climb the career ladder but whose circumstances preclude higher education would be spared spending fruitless years in university running up debt.

Universities are expensive to run because they are pre-industrial craft industries in which productivity gains are rare. They find it difficult to control their costs and rely instead on increasing their income by enrolling more students. This business model has made Australian universities among the largest in the world, but the quality of the education they provide has suffered. The ratio of staff to students has deteriorated, and tutorials barely exist.

Because admission-qualified students already attend university, expanding enrolments requires lowering admission standards. Universities have nothing to lose by admitting poorly prepared students (and failing to provide them with remedial support) because the institutions keep the fees even when dropouts and graduates fail to repay their student loans. Although the graduate premium is shrinking, marginal students continue to enrol in universities because they also have little financial risk; taxpayers pick up the cost of their unpaid loans.

Degree inflation and the perverse incentives of the funding system have combined to blight the life chances of many members of the young generation. Without any change, student debt will continue to mount, large amounts of capital will be misallocated, and social mobility will remain stalled. It is time for a policy reset.

A just distribution of risk, subsidies and resources would benefit students from disadvantaged backgrounds as well as the wider society. Perhaps the biggest challenge of all is the reinvigoration of the cultural, moral, and character-building functions of higher education. It is not easy to challenge the myth that universities exist solely for economic advancement, but it is worth trying.

All Shall Have Degrees

Australia's university system, born from egalitarian ideals in 1850, has transformed from educating a select elite to mass credential production. Post-WWII expansion accelerated as degrees became viewed as economic productivity boosters. Policy changes like the Dawkins reforms and demand-driven funding turbocharged growth — domestic enrolments increased 70% since 2001, master's degrees tripled, and half of young Australians now hold degrees. This expansion came at vocational education's expense, with TAFE stigmatised as universities became $100 billion enterprises. Yet universities still demand more growth despite evidence questioning its societal benefits.

Dollars for Degrees

The graduate premium — earnings advantage over non-graduates — has shrunk from 25% above average wages in the 1990s to just 15% today, with Australia now having the OECD's third-smallest premium. For bottom-quintile graduates across disciplines, skipping university would yield higher lifetime earnings. Postgraduate degrees are becoming the new inflation frontier, with master's premiums halving. This credential inflation creates a vicious cycle where more degrees are required for the same jobs, trapping those unable to access higher education while burdening many graduates with debt for credentials of diminishing value.

Graduates and Growth

The assumed link between graduate numbers and GDP growth proves tenuous at best. International comparisons show no consistent relationship, with some high-education countries having lower per-capita GDP. Wages reflect national wealth more than individual productivity — Kenyan bus drivers don't suddenly become more productive when working in Germany. The signaling theory explains this paradox: degrees indicate pre-existing traits rather than creating human capital. As credentials proliferate, their signaling value erodes, requiring ever-higher qualifications for the same jobs.

The Business of Universities

Behind their scholarly veneer, universities operate as prestige-maximising businesses. They suffer from Baumol's cost disease — with limited productivity gains possible in handcrafted education — requiring constant revenue growth through expanded enrolments. The HELP loan system creates moral hazard: students borrow excessively knowing taxpayers bear default risk, while universities admit marginal students without accountability for outcomes. TEQSA's rigid accreditation enforces conformity, stifling innovation that could improve quality and reduce costs.

Policy Recommendations

1. Where feasible, drop degree requirements for jobs. Overnight, the value of professional societies, vocational schools, online educators, specialised training, and the military would be enhanced.
2. The esteem of VET would also be improved by combining it with

higher education and allowing students to include VET subjects in their degrees.

3. Reduce regressive subsidies and ensure that universities and students carry more of the risk of non-repayment.
4. Reform regulation and accreditation to encourage innovation and experimentation rather than conformity.
5. Brilliant academics represent Australia's finest intellects, but we cannot expect to find a world-beating genius standing in front of every lecture theatre. For most academic staff, teaching should be their job — rather than research — and doing it well should be the basis of their career progression.

Conclusion

Australia's mass higher education experiment has reached diminishing returns. What began as an engine of social mobility now exacerbates inequality while delivering questionable economic benefits. Restoring universities' cultural and character-forming missions while curtailing credential inflation can make higher education both more valuable and more just. As Flannery O'Connor noted, we must push as hard as the age pushing against us - now is the time to rethink higher education's purpose beyond mere credentialism.

> This is a summary of a Centre for Independent Studies research paper. The full paper can be found at https://www.cis.org.au/publication/degree-inflation-undermining-the-value-of-higher-education/

39

Déjà Vu in Australian Higher Education

Steven Schwartz

History repeats itself, often with a sense of irony only those with long memories can fully appreciate. In a move evocative of a plot twist in a rather predictable novel, the Australian government is resurrecting a centralised body much like the Tertiary Education Commission (TEC) it once enthusiastically dismantled. This time, they promise it will be better, shinier, and more centralised, with control over university admissions, funding, and maybe even what brand of pencils academics can use.

The original TEC was born in the 1970s, when flared pants were fashionable and bureaucratic behemoths were seen as the solution to every problem. The TEC was supposed to bring order and equality to higher education. Instead, it became a lumbering dinosaur, choking on red tape and inefficiency until the government, in a rare moment of clarity, decided to pull the plug in the 1980s. Innovation was the new mantra, and universities were to be liberated from the shackles of central control.

Fast-forward to today, and the government seems to have forgotten why it axed the TEC in the first place. The new body, the Australian Tertiary Education Commission (ATEC), promises to iron out all those pesky disparities in funding, ensure standardised equality across the board, and generally make everything peachy. Sounds great, right? Except it's not.

Here's the thing about centralised bodies: they are the antithesis of innovation. Bureaucrats, bless their hearts, are excellent at creating mountains of paperwork and taking eons to respond to emails but not so great at fostering creativity or responding swiftly to change. The only thing they standardise is mediocrity.

What we need in higher education is not more control but more competition. Think about it. Giving universities the freedom to innovate allows them to tailor their offerings to meet the needs of their students and their communities. They can experiment with new teaching methods, collaborate with industries, and develop cutting-edge research without waiting for a nod from some distant bureaucratic overlord.

Australia already has a Tertiary Education Quality Assurance Agency (TEQSA), a Soviet-style bureaucracy that generates mountains of paperwork, takes months to answer even a simple query, and whose staff spend most of their time on training courses. No one believes that TEQSA has improved the quality of Australian higher education, least of all the students. Will TEQSA be disbanded? Don't be naïve. ATEC will not replace TEQSA; universities will have to deal with both.

Given the new body promises to oversee funding allocations, admissions policies, and possibly even curriculum standards, there will be considerable latitude for duplication with TEQSA. Adding another layer of bureaucracy with overlapping functions is like hiring a second gardener to mow the same lawn. It's redundant, confusing, and a waste of resources. Bureaucracies have an insidious way of growing beyond their original remit, gobbling up funds and time as they expand their control.

Competition, on the other hand, drives improvement. When universities compete for students, funding, and prestige, they are motivated to offer the best possible education and services. Competition leads to a diverse ecosystem of institutions, each with unique strengths and specialisations, catering to a wide range of needs and preferences.

Imagine if our universities were free to compete on a level playing field. They could develop niche programs, partner with local businesses for hands-on training, and create unique learning environments. Students would benefit from a broader array of choices, and employers would have access to graduates with various skills and experiences.

Innovation flourishes in an environment where institutions are encouraged to take risks and try new things. This dynamism propels industries forward and keeps them relevant. Higher education should be no different.

Instead of resurrecting the TEC, let's dismantle the barriers to competition. Reduce the regulatory burden on universities and let them operate with the autonomy needed to adapt and thrive. Provide transparency in outcomes so students can make informed choices about where to study based on the quality and relevance of the education offered. Support universities in their efforts to innovate and excel rather than tying them up in bureaucratic red tape.

As Karl Marx famously observed, "History repeats itself, first as tragedy, second as farce". Let's not allow the revival of the TEC to become a farce. Instead, let's champion a system that values competition, fosters innovation, and ultimately serves the needs of students and society far better than any centralised control ever could.

This opinion piece was originally published by *The Spectator*.

40

A Shorter Path to Teaching

Rob Joseph

Over the past 40 years, Initial Teacher Education (ITE) in Australia has transitioned from being delivered in teaching colleges to universities, with increasing formalisation of qualifications and standards, particularly following the 2004 NSW Teacher Accreditation Act and the establishment of AITSL in 2009. The one-year Graduate Diploma in Education (DipEd) was once a popular postgraduate entry into teaching, but from 2014 it was phased out in favour of a two-year Master's program, formalised by AITSL's 2015 accreditation standards. By 2016, the DipEd had been discontinued. This shift was inspired by international comparisons, particularly Finland, although the rationale for the change was not thoroughly documented.

Australia faces major teacher workforce challenges, especially in STEM subjects and rural schools. In recent years, the number of commencing Initial Teacher Education (ITE) students has been lower in most jurisdictions than in previous times. Australia's education ministers are in the process of producing a series of actions to address teacher workforce challenges — including both recruitment and retention. It is likely that a range of policy measures will be required to sufficiently meet these challenges.

One key policy measure that could support improved teacher supply is the (re)creation of one-year postgraduate teaching pathways. Until recently, the one-year Graduate Diploma in Education (the 'DipEd') was the most popular postgraduate option for ITE. It is estimated around 60,000 of Australia's teachers hold a DipEd. However, coinciding with a 2014 review, this one-year qualification was phased out, and a new requirement was introduced mandating postgraduate ITE programs be equivalent to at least two years of full-time study. This means prospective postgraduate

ITE students are required to complete a two-year qualification, rather than one year.

The evidence base for this decision was weak and poorly documented. It appears no consideration was given to research showing a mixed relationship between length of pre-service training and teacher effectiveness, nor to international examples of high-achieving education systems that offer one-year teaching pathways.

Additionally, since the policy change took place, a range of measures has been introduced to boost standards for graduating teachers — including academic entry thresholds, literacy and numeracy tests, and teacher performance assessments. If the rationale for the two-year requirement was to increase standards, this reason has now been addressed through other policy initiatives.

The two-year requirement is a major disincentive for mid-career professionals looking to become teachers, as it represents a doubling of their student debt, foregone income, and time spent balancing study, work, and family commitments. Multiple reviews have recommended removing this two-year requirement, including the Commonwealth Government's Quality Initial Teacher Education Review (September 2022), the NSW Productivity Commission's White Paper (June 2021), and the NSW Legislative Council education committee's Report of the inquiry into teacher shortages in New South Wales (November 2022). The policy has also been supported by the Federal Opposition, Catholic Schools NSW, and many principals and teachers.

The authority for any changes in this policy area lies with each state or territory's Teacher Regulatory Authority (TRA), which manages accreditation of ITE programs at universities within their jurisdiction. Although some TRAs have linked the approval of ITE programs to national standards (set by AITSL), in other jurisdictions, TRAs could lift the two-year requirement, allowing local universities to offer one-year pathways.

At a federal level, the Australian Institute for Teaching and School Leadership (AITSL) sets national or agreed cross-jurisdictional accreditation standards for ITE programs. AITSL lifting their two-year requirement would encourage individual TRAs to follow suit. Though not sufficient on its own, creating a standards-based one-year postgraduate teaching pathway is an important and necessary step to help improve Australia's teacher supply.

Teacher shortages

Concerns about teacher shortages—especially in STEM subjects and rural schools—have intensified. A 2021 AITSL report found that Mathematics is taught by out-of-field teachers 40% of the time, and rural schools report higher vacancy rates than metropolitan schools. While some argue that shortages are localised, federal modelling anticipates a shortfall of 4,100 secondary teachers by 2025. Although some contest the scale of the problem, low ITE completion rates (55% undergraduate, 76% postgraduate) are a pressing concern. Governments are therefore seeking ways to increase both enrolments and completions.

Calls for one-year pathways

Several government reviews and inquiries have supported a return to one-year postgraduate teaching programs. The 2021 QITE Review suggested recognising the prior learning of skilled mid-career changers to allow a one-year qualification. Similarly, the NSW Productivity Commission and the NSW Legislative Council have recommended models that integrate one year of study with one year of in-school placement. Catholic Schools NSW and the federal Coalition have also backed reinstating one-year pathways, citing the need to attract more candidates into the profession.

Disincentives of two-year requirement

The two-year Master's requirement deters many prospective teachers, especially mid-career changers, due to the doubled tuition cost and lost income. Surveys have shown these individuals often underestimate the course length and are discouraged by financial and time constraints. Research from the Behavioural Economics Team of the Australian Government (BETA) found that a one-year ITE course was as appealing as a $20,000 pay rise, illustrating its strong appeal. Postgraduate ITE completion rates have declined since the one-year programs were removed, unlike other postgraduate fields.

Limited evidence base for two-year requirement

There is little evidence supporting the effectiveness of longer ITE programs. Research shows that higher teacher qualifications do not necessarily improve student outcomes, and that attributes such as subject expertise and training quality are more reliable indicators of teacher effectiveness. Finland, often cited as justification for Australia's policy change, has seen declining PISA results, while countries like Singapore maintain high performance with one-year programs. Furthermore, there is no evidence that teachers with one-year qualifications perform worse, despite tens of thousands having been trained via this route.

No change in standards

Reintroducing one-year teaching pathways would not lower standards. It would simply amend the length of study under current accreditation frameworks. Existing quality controls — such as the LANTITE, TPAs, academic entry requirements, and professional development obligations — would remain in place. In fact, many of these measures were introduced after the phase-out of one-year programs, meaning any new pathway would be subject to stricter oversight than previous versions.

A continuum of standards

Teaching quality is now assessed through a standards-based continuum — Graduate, Proficient, Highly Accomplished, and Lead — rather than being solely determined at the point of entry. New teachers develop over time through mentoring and ongoing training. This structured model, overseen by statutory bodies like NESA and VIT, highlights that initial training length is less important than the teacher's demonstrated professional practice.

Building on existing flexibility

Several states already offer flexible, employment-based pathways into teaching that allow students to work while studying. Programs like Turn to Teaching (QLD), Mid-Career Transition to Teaching (NSW), and Teach for Australia demonstrate that high standards can be maintained within flexible frameworks. Some universities also offer fast-tracked two-year Master's programs in 18 months, though these still retain many of the original disincentives.

Options for one-year postgraduate qualifications

Multiple models could support a one-year teaching pathway, including a reinstated Graduate Diploma in Education, or qualifications limited to secondary or hard-to-staff areas such as STEM and rural schools. Accelerated and employment-based programs also offer partial solutions, but a straightforward return to a one-year postgraduate qualification would be more impactful. States could lead this reform by allowing universities to offer one-year programs within their jurisdictions, potentially under a revised qualification title that reflects today's standards-based environment.

Conclusion

Amid growing teacher shortages and declining ITE completions, introducing a one-year postgraduate pathway would be a practical and effective response. There is minimal evidence supporting the current two-year model, while many high-performing education systems already use shorter pathways. Australia's own history with the DipEd, the strong support among policymakers and educators, and robust current accreditation standards all suggest a well-regulated one-year pathway could safely return. The change requires no new laws or funding and could be implemented quickly by states or led by AITSL. It represents a rare 'quick win' in public policy to address a critical workforce issue.

Appendix

Comparison of course structure between diploma and masters in ITE

Sample comparison for a student aspiring to teach Chemistry in secondary schools.

	Graduate Diploma *University of Technology Sydney (UTS) 2004 | 8x classes*	**Masters** *University of Technology Sydney (UTS) 2021 | 16x classes*
Core units	Professional Practice in the Secondary School	Understanding and Engaging Adolescent Learners
	Psychology of Secondary Students	Learning Futures: Teaching for Complexity and Diversity
	Professional Practice in Catering for Difference and Special Needs	Professional Learning
	Social and Philosophical Aspects of Secondary Education	Literacy and Numeracy Across the Curriculum
		Inclusive Education
		Teaching and Learning with Digital Technologies
		Resetting the Future: Indigenous Australian Education
Curriculum units	Learning in Science 1	Science Teaching Methods 1
	Learning in Science 2	Chemistry Teaching Methods 2
	Professional Practice in Science 1	Chemistry Teaching Methods 3
	Professional Practice in Science 2	*Professional Experience Teaching Practice 1*
		Professional Experience Teaching Practice 2
Elective units		*Choose 4, for example:*
		Teaching Across the Curriculum
		Aboriginal Sydney Now
		Education: Rights and Responsibilities
		Create: Creating Interactive Multimedia Objects

This is a summary of a Centre for Independent Studies research paper. The full paper can be found at https://www.cis.org.au/publication/a-shorter-path-to-teaching-exploring-one-year-postgraduate-qualifications/

41

Eliminating the F-Word:
No More Failure?

Steven Schwartz

By preventing students from experiencing failure, we will keep them from gaining the self-confidence that comes from overcoming it.

British politician Enoch Powell famously said "All political lives end in failure"— a proposition amply corroborated by his own career. Scholars are vulnerable to a similar fate. To paraphrase the famous anthropologist Marshall Sahlins, academics can be certain of two things: someday, they will all be dead, and eventually, they will all be proven wrong. (Sahlins' tip for a successful scholarly career: make sure the first precedes the second.)

Even superstars fail. In a classic Nike advertisement, basketball legend Michael Jordan confesses to missing more than 9,000 shots and losing almost 300 basketball games in his career. "Twenty-six times," he says, "I've been trusted to take the game-winning shot—and missed. I've failed over and over again in my life". Then he delivers the line that has attracted millions of people to view the ad on *YouTube*: "And that is why I succeed".

Jordan's message is motivating and inspiring, but it's also worrying. If failure is essential to success, then what are the prospects for our current crop of students who have never experienced failure of any kind? No school student is held back, summer school repeats are rare, and first-class honours are becoming the typical university grade. What happens when these students move out of education, where success is now the norm, to a world in which failure is ubiquitous? Never having had to deal with setbacks, never having failed at anything, will they have the capacity to cope? We will soon find out.

Over the past 20 years, government policy has resulted in an avalanche of university students. The highest-ranked institutions swept up the best-prepared applicants, forcing the less prestigious universities to lower their entry standards drastically. Not surprisingly, many of these poorly-prepared students are finding themselves unable to complete their courses; dropout rates have climbed to record levels.

Under the rules governing accreditation, Australian universities have a legal requirement to ensure that the students they admit have the educational background and study support to complete their courses. It appears that universities have flaunted this requirement, so the government has stepped in.

In a daring display of its unshakeable commitment to the academic success of its constituents, the federal government has introduced legislation that could revolutionise, or perhaps obliterate, the way we understand the concept of failure. Call it the 'No Student Left Behind — Especially If They've Failed' Act. It's an ambitious move, guaranteeing the total eradication of that ghastly 'F' word from the Australian educational system: failure.

The Australian government is mandating that university students who score less than 50% in their exams shall be entitled to a slew of educational life-savers. University-funded tutoring, counselling, examination do-overs, special exams, and extended deadlines are all on the table. With these bountiful resources at their disposal, no student will ever feel the sting of failure again. And to ensure universities are as invested in the success of their students as the government, a hefty fine of $18,780 per student will be introduced for those institutions that fail to help their students rise above the 50 per cent benchmark.

If Dante were alive, he might have added a tenth circle to his 'Inferno' for the university administrators who will have to deal with this fiscal sword of Damocles. Instead of cramming more students into lecture halls and labs, universities will have to find funds for an army of tutors, counsellors, and exam monitors.

But worry not, for the Education Minister has spoken: "Universities should be helping students to succeed, not to fail". It's a comforting thought, almost reminiscent of a fairy tale ending. It gives students a cosy sense of assurance that the government is there, always ready to sweep in and replace the big bad wolf of failure with the benevolent fairy godmother of success. But will it work?

Tim Harford fears it won't. In his book, *Adapt: Why Success Always Follows Failure,* Harford claims that messing up is central to learning. Students gain more from mistakes, blind alleys and dead ends than from success. Failures give students the opportunity to 'pick themselves up, dust themselves off and start all over again'.

Such resilience is essential because becoming an expert is a long process, at least 10,000 hours, says Malcolm Gladwell in *Outliers.* Expertise takes a long time to acquire because, outside of universities, 50 per cent is not good enough. The real world has higher standards. Businesses will collapse if their accountants are only 50 per cent accurate, computer programs that work only half the time are useless, and no one would be happy if surgeons fluffed half their operations. A 10,000-hour apprenticeship provides plenty of opportunities for students to learn from their errors, and everyone knows that practice makes perfect.

Failing is not only essential to honing one's skills, but it also provides the chance to cultivate oneself ('Whatever doesn't kill you makes you stronger'). The character traits forged by experiencing and overcoming failure are necessary for success in any field. Tenaciousness, resilience, drive, perseverance and the ability to delay gratification while working toward a distant goal are just as crucial in achieving success as intelligence. Psychologist Angela Lee Duckworth calls this combination of character traits "grit". It comes from confronting failure and overcoming it. Without failure, progress is impossible.

Universities, faced with high costs and potential fines, may be tempted to take the easy way out and pass every single student. That view might sound cynical, but it is realistic. Will a university degree retain its lustre when passing becomes an expected, almost mundane occurrence rather than a reward for hard work, grit, and resilience? If everyone is a winner, is anyone winning anything at all?

But these are long-term concerns, and our politicians are unable to think beyond the next election campaign. They look forward to offering voters a world where failure ceases to exist, and success requires no effort. A world in which every student gets a degree just for showing up.

It's an idyllic vision that might catch on across the globe. Imagine a future in which everyone gets a shot at the Grand Dream, even if their exam scores are below 50 per cent, a time in which the 'School of Hard Knocks' has shut its doors forever. Fans of Horatio Alger novels, the stoic pioneers who defined the ethos of hard work and success through perseverance, must be turning in their graves.

The moral of the story, dear reader, is that university failure is on the brink of extinction. At least, it is Down Under. This extraordinary development will have vast repercussions for education, success, and the very nature of our universities.

Of course, we want our students to succeed. But passing every student will ensure just the opposite. By preventing students from experiencing failure, we will keep them from gaining the self-confidence that comes from overcoming it.

If we want young people to be able to handle life's inevitable slings and arrows, then for their own sake, we must let them fail.

This opinion piece was originally published by *The Spectator.*

SECTION 6

Funding Reform and the Politics of Money

Few issues in Australian education generate more noise — or less measurable progress — than school funding. For over a decade, debates have revolved around how much money schools should receive, how it should be distributed, and which level of government should pay. This section examines the persistent belief that more money equals better education, and the hard truth that outcomes have stubbornly failed to improve despite record-breaking increases in funding.

In *Education Policy Must Mature Beyond Calls for More Money*, Glenn Fahey takes aim at the dominant political narrative: that education is underfunded and only in need of additional investment to thrive. He points out that Australia already ranks among the world's highest spenders on schooling. The problem, he argues, is not how much we spend, but how poorly we spend it. Fahey criticises needs-based funding mechanisms that assume equity can be achieved by redistributing teachers, rather than improving the quality of teaching itself. He warns that without clear, enforceable performance targets, national reform agreements risk becoming expensive gestures rather than engines of educational improvement.

This argument is sharpened in *How Not to Waste Gonski School Funding* by Trisha Jha. Analysing the latest iteration of 'Gonski-inspired' deals, Jha notes that an additional $16 billion in federal funding has been promised under the new Better and Fairer Schools Agreement, with vague language and limited accountability. While there are some hopeful developments — such as national support for explicit instruction and early phonics screening — Jha warns that states are rewarded for delay, political negotiation overrides policy coherence, and critical terms like "evidence-based" remain dangerously undefined. Without consequences for non-delivery, she predicts that in ten years we may again be asking why the money made so little difference.

Both authors are clear: more money is not a reform strategy. The lesson of the past decade is that funding without focus delivers diminishing returns. Real reform requires not just more resources but sharper priorities: a laser focus on teacher quality, stronger incentives for measurable results, and the political courage to spend less on what's fashionable and more on what works.

42

Education Policy Must Mature Beyond Calls for More Money

Glenn Fahey

Education policy must mature from being dominated by demands for more funding and instead focus on delivering better outcomes and greater accountability.

This week saw the first of the new funding deals between Canberra and the states: the renegotiation of so-called 'national school reform agreements'. In announcing the $774m deal with Western Australia, Education Minister Jason Clare confirmed Canberra will add $3b a year to its current annual tab of around $23b (around 2.5 times what it was in 2009).

This comes off the back of a pivotal December meeting of education ministers, where Clare presented an ambitious roadmap to the states that would not only bring more money, but also more accountability and shared commitment to better outcomes. But it's clear the states had successfully scaled back the targets proposed by Clare so that what remained were fewer in number and more modest in scope.

Unfortunately, states are now competing to out-lobby each other in extracting more funding from Canberra (with little mention of their own funding contributions, or lack thereof). As this week's negotiation shows, states may be able to secure this additional funding with little mention of obligations to meet Canberra's targets.

Unsatisfied with Clare's latest round of investment, education unions have already accused the government of "underfunding", despite Australian school resourcing being already among the highest and fastest-increasing in the developed world.

This will be a real test of the government's resolve: is it genuinely committed to resetting relations with the states and simply using funding increases as a bargaining sweetener? Or are we witnessing more of the same, where education politics trumps policy?

There are two specific issues at play: first that the role of targets will be watered down, with more funding to end up coming with few or no strings, and second that additional funding will go to the wrong places.

These issues echo mistakes from the Gillard era funding reforms that Clare mustn't repeat. Gonski's 2011 review provided a seemingly robust and consistent new school funding formula. But in the end, it arguably became little more than cover for the pre-determined political goal of pumping more money into schools.

Since the last round of major funding reform, states and unions successfully campaigned for more funding — but the Gonski approach to funding has since proven to have been misguided.

The current needs-based funding logic is simple: if a school has more disadvantaged students, it gets more public money. That extra funding is used, often, to hire more teachers to allow for smaller class sizes — in theory giving students more and better access to learn.

However, the problem is that this logic is flawed. Decades of evidence show that it's not more teachers that produces better results, but the quality of the teaching inside classrooms. For this reason, needs-based funding can only work if it is used not to redistribute the number of teachers in the system, but the quality of teaching available to students.

Rather than more funding being pumped in across-the-board, it should make the most effective teachers available to the very neediest of students. This is an important example of the fact that, to be successful, additional Commonwealth funding must come with commitment to meaningful targets.

A lot of good work has been done in recent years to offer a genuine pathway for identifying and using performance targets. If taken seriously, this would reset the role of education's federal-state relations from being simply another funding handout and instead towards more concretely promoting shared goals of lifting education outcomes.

The Productivity Commission concluded that previous funding rounds had done little to improve outcomes — warning policy had become vague, bureaucratic and lost sight of the end goal. And, in its December report, the 'Better and Fairer' review recommended a suite of reform actions and expected outcome measures to improve accountability and shift performance in schools and systems.

Put simply, the greatest outcomes that matter in education systems are how well those systems help students to keep up, catch up, and move up in their literacy and numeracy proficiencies. Targets must unapologetically align with this.

It is not enough to simply tie funding to the latest educational fad: this risks creating more educational white elephants. The former Labor government's Building the Education Revolution (countless empty school halls) and the Digital Education Revolution (buying up more laptops per student than anywhere in the world at the time) proved to be costly and ineffective.

To this end, although it's welcome that Clare has promised to only spend new money on evidence-backed projects, caution should still be taken with some proposed projects. Massively ramping up small-group tutoring in schools is a worthy objective, but is not yet supported with what's needed to be delivered with maximum effect.

And while admirable in intent, the effort to promote students' wellbeing on par with their academics is likely to backfire and risks pumping up a new industry of providers spruiking evidence-free approaches across Australia's schools.

To date, the Albanese government has proven capable of promoting genuine education policy reform. Clare has a privileged opportunity to shape education policy for the next decade, but the decisions in steering the new school reform agreements this year will be decisive.

This opinion piece was originally published by *The Australian*.

43

How Not to Waste Gonski School Funding

Trisha Jha

A federal election was looming, a budget was imminent, and the Prime Minister had declared that, for Labor, "nothing is more important to building Australia's future than education".

In the interests of dulling the school funding headache, federal education minister Jason Clare offered more money than originally promised — in what is claimed to be the final piece of the Gonski funding puzzle — to get the new Better and Fairer Schools Agreement across the line. Clare spent 2024 promising $16 billion of additional funding for schools, in return for improvement and implementation on key metrics and policies.

But the year ended with Western Australia, Tasmania, the ACT and NT signing on, while bigger states held out. That recalcitrance has been rewarded. Deals signed with Victoria and South Australia in January doubled the increase in the federal contribution to the Schooling Resource Standard (SRS) from 22.5% to 25%. Holdouts Queensland and New South Wales will demand the same, Western Australia has already signed on for the extra, and you can expect the remaining jurisdictions to follow.

With Opposition Leader Peter Dutton committing in January to match the government dollar-for-dollar, this funding is as good as locked in for the next 10 years — so it's worth examining what the return on investment might be. History is a guide, but it doesn't lead us to be particularly optimistic.

The previous five-year National School Reform Agreement lifted federal funding to 20% of the SRS, but — as the Productivity Commission's 2022 review noted — failed to meaningfully improve student outcomes. Many of the problems facing Australian education have simply become more apparent since then. Roughly a third of students across all subjects and year levels are failing to meet NAPLAN proficiency, and OECD testing shows today's 15-year-olds have declined relative to those in 2000 — a year behind in science, a year and a half in reading, and almost two years in mathematics.

It's also hard to improve student learning outcomes if they're turning up less than they used to. The most recent data shows a decade ago, overall school attendance for Year 7-10 was over 90%. It has since fallen five percentage points. Student attendance levels — the proportion of children who attend school 90% of the time — have also fallen.

Year 12 retention is going backwards, and students who stay are increasingly taking up less demanding options. For instance, in 2022, 10% of Victorian students doing their VCE opted to go 'unscored', meaning they did not sit exams and did not receive an ATAR — more than double the proportion in 2018.

Further, high-level policy change can only work to improve student outcomes if it directly impacts classroom practice. And — though this is controversial — it's students' engagement in learning, and whether they are safe and well at school, that should be the focus of education policy. Get students learning in disruption-free classrooms, and many of the other outcomes will follow.

The good news is that many Australian governments have become more focused on classroom practice. The bad news is the language in the Agreement is in many cases too vague to effectively hold education systems to account.

However, almost every state and territory has adopted their own policy around evidence-based reading instruction, and the Agreement requires a nationally-consistent Year 1 Phonics Check. Early intervention is on the agenda with similar numeracy checks, and support for students who fall behind through a "multi-tiered systems of support".

Explicit instruction — used in some of our most successful schools — is also increasingly embraced as an evidence-based approach to teaching that aligns with the evidence on how students learn; and is also a powerful tool for improving educational equity. Some Catholic dioceses — educating a sizeable minority of Australian students — are also embedding these practices in their schools.

Now, the less good news. Explicit instruction works best when paired with a curriculum that is knowledge-focused, coherent and consolidated across time in school. The Australian Curriculum in its current form does not support schools to deliver this for all students. A future federal government should do what it can to fix this.

Contrary to popular belief, the Agreement also does not mandate explicit instruction, just "evidence-based teaching", and there is deep disagreement about what constitutes 'evidence'. As for the promise of early intervention, the devil is in the detail. For instance, WA's bilateral agreement doesn't necessarily mean its public schools will do anything new in numeracy screening.

Additional federal money may unfortunately extend and expand inefficient and ineffective practices — such as small-group tutoring programs — rather than the more difficult task of lifting the quality of whole-class instruction across 9,000+ schools. Most significantly, all the targets and initiatives in this agreement can only work if there's a consequence for not following through. That would take a very brave Canberra.

More likely, we will be back here in 10 years ... wondering why we have little to show for the investment.

This opinion piece was originally published by the Australian Financial Review.

44

Dollars And Sense: Time For Smart Reform of Australia's School Funding

Glenn Fahey

Australia is among the highest-spending countries on schooling in the world. Yet the educational return on this investment — for parents, taxpayers, employers, and students — has deteriorated.

Australia has continued to increase funding, despite international research long showing little to no relationship between resourcing and achievement. More than $61 billion of public funding is spent on schooling each year in Australia. The average public funding per student is just under $16,000 — a 17 per cent real increase since 2009. It's a myth that funding has been cut — even the rate of increase in funding is growing.

Australia's international performance in PISA testing has been "steadily negative" according to the OECD, and in domestic testing, overall achievement in NAPLAN has remained flat. International comparisons show a lack of funding can't be blamed for Australia's educational decline. There are high-performing countries (such as Estonia, Poland, New Zealand, Ireland, Hong Kong, Canada, Japan, and Taiwan) that spend around 24 per cent less per student over the course of a student's typical time in the school system.

More Funding Hasn't Improved Student Achievement

Analysis of school-level data (all primary government schools in Australia) shows the expensive Gonski funding model has not resulted in higher student achievement.

There is no statistical relationship between increased public funding and student achievement. If two schools with comparable cohorts of students, but different funding levels, are randomly selected, those schools' students would perform roughly the same on average.

Student achievement in Year 5 NAPLAN is mostly explained by other in-school and out-of-school factors.

- The best predictors of student achievement in year 5 are students' past achievement (year 3) and their socio-educational background (as indicated by the Index of Community Socio-Educational Advantage (ICSEA)).
- The attendance rate (the average proportion of days that students attend school) and the level of funding voluntarily paid by parents are also statistically significant, but relatively weak in terms of their effect size.

Australian Education Isn't Underfunded. It's Been Directed to the Wrong Priorities

Expensive policy approaches, such as reductions to class sizes and increases to across-the-board teacher salaries, which have been tried for decades, haven't delivered educational benefits.

Australian teachers' salaries are:

- Relatively high compared to other countries;
- Relatively high compared with other tertiary-educated workers (particularly for women);
- Increasing more than twice as quickly as the OECD average;
- Very flat over time — peaking early in their careers;
- Mostly based on central determination in awards;
- Not related to performance, but to years of service and credentials.

Class sizes (as approximated by student-teacher ratios) have effectively halved since the 1960s, which has been responsible for much of the additional cost of schooling. There is no evidence that smaller classes lead to better learning of students. In fact, the OECD now indicates students in larger classes outperform those in smaller classes, on average.

Modestly increasing class size by just one student could save around $360 per student (or around $1.4 billion). This saving could be used to compensate financial incentives for high-performing teachers — meaning a better investment in teachers' capacity rather than simply increasing teacher numbers.

There is no evidence that recent efforts to expand 'needs-based' funding are properly targeted in a way that will achieve the objective of reducing educational disadvantage and lift education outcomes.

The school funding formula approach is too broadly applied to genuinely meet the needs of disadvantaged students.

We Must Make Better Investment in Our Teachers

The most significant financial investment the education system makes is in its teachers. The only way to sustainably improve education outcomes is to further develop the capacity of teachers. Boosting the quality of teaching is by far the best way to improve students' educational outcomes. For resourcing to improve student achievement, the school funding approach should specifically support incentives for high performance of teachers.

The relatively flat structure and inflexibility make it harder to retain high-ability teachers. Approaches to boost the quality of the teaching workforce should focus on increasing, rather than decreasing, the supply of potential teachers. More competition for teaching positions will lift standards.

- Expanding access to teaching can be provided with more flexible pathways to become a teacher, supported by on-the-job training.
- More flexible, demand-based salaries — based on subject area shortages, hard-to-service areas, and having specialist skills — will better meet needs of the teaching workforce.

Confused approaches to teacher workforce development, and additional credentialisation have harmed, rather than helped, the status of the teaching profession.

Policymakers have let teachers and school leaders down by failing to provide the necessary tools for performance management practices needed to build capacity and providing a supportive incentive structure.

- o Current approaches to recognise effective teachers are not working.
- o There are few opportunities for genuine performance management in schools — with limited independent classroom observations, performance monitoring, and feedback.
- o Teachers' performance appraisals rarely result in rewards or development opportunities — with school leaders unable to recognise high performers.
- o Poor performance management is a key reason teachers leave the profession.
- o Teachers report that underperformance is regularly tolerated and goes unaddressed — with school leaders unable to dismiss underperformers.
- o School leaders would benefit from more discretion with performance management, rather than working within bureaucratic.

Improving the Approach to School Funding Could Turn Things Around

Rather than the amount of funding, the approach itself may be responsible for poor educational outcomes and failing to align incentives toward higher performance.

Australia's school funding approach is:

- o Based on a flawed methodology;
- o highly centralised;
- o overly complex, opaque, and indirect;
- o input-based rather than outcomes-based; and
- o not designed to promote school choice and competition.

The input-based approach means funding is based on who comes to a school (number of students and their demographics) rather than what happens at a school. A more outcomes-based approach reorients funding based on activity and the quality of education that schools deliver. This includes funding that directly ties to individual or school indicators for performance.

Performance-based pay is shown to increase teachers' motivation, increase parents' confidence in schools, improve productivity, improve teaching methods and teachers' responsiveness to students' learning needs.

Research shows several design features can make performance incentives effective in practice:

- being supported by broader professional development practices (though including financial incentives is effective on its own, even without the benefit of further performance management);
- when multiple measures of performance are used (including, but not exclusively, student achievement);
- where the incentive payments are relatively high (at or above a 7.5 per cent bonus);
- where duration is longer (more than 3 years);
- and especially beneficial when attached to achievement scores in mathematics.
- Focussed on individual performance, rather than school-based performance.

Australia's various school systems are funded through increasingly complex formulas, but the underlying methodology is based on flawed premises. It's based on the past funding of relatively high-achieving schools, not the efficient cost of providing quality education.

A technical and independent evaluation of both the evidence supporting the Gonski review and the effectiveness of subsequent funding increases should be delegated to the National School Resourcing Board. Current oversight is limited to compliance with legislation, rather than the quality of spending and education delivered.

School funding is indirect and not transparent to parents and taxpayers. It would be better if funding were provided directly to households through means-tested vouchers, rather than going through systems that redistribute funding and result in poor alignment between funding and student needs.

School decision-making is highly centralised, limiting school-level autonomy and accountability. There is scope for deregulating school spending decisions in Australia, which will improve efficiency, and result in better outcomes for students. There should be more meaningful ways for parents to support schools in decision-making, such as through school governing boards and other school types (like charter schools) that empower local decision-making and less bureaucracy.

Market-based accountability through choice and competition can more efficiently allocated resources. Research shows more competition increases school performance, and transparent reporting of school outcomes is related to higher student achievement. School choice actually reduces, rather than increases, inequity in education. There are several policy options available to expand school choice alternatives — such as bursaries for students in low income households to use at non-government schools.

> This is a summary of a Centre for Independent Studies research paper. The full paper can be found at https://www.cis.org.au/publication/dollars-and-sense-time-for-smart-reform-of-australian-school-funding/

Epilogue:
Reform That Works

Australia's education sector has become a paradox: awash with resources, ambition, and reform proposals—yet delivering outcomes that are, at best, underwhelming. Despite more than a decade of inquiries, funding boosts, and curriculum rewrites, our international performance has flatlined or declined. Our students are not less capable. Our schools are not worse. But our policy settings are misaligned.

The essays in this book converge around a quiet but powerful idea: education policy must stop treating ideology as evidence and rediscover the fundamentals of what works.

What does that mean?

First, it means reclaiming teaching from fads and philosophies. The science of learning tells us that students benefit from explicit instruction, frequent review, and cumulative practice. Yet too many schools adopt discovery learning, inquiry models, or "constructivist" approaches unsupported by robust evidence.

Second, it means recognising that early intervention is not a slogan, but a system. Screening in literacy and numeracy should be universal and backed by evidence-based remediation. These are low-cost, high-impact reforms that can radically reduce disadvantage over time.

Third, it means holding institutions accountable for outcomes, not just intentions. Schools and universities that fail to deliver on core learning goals should face real consequences, not just revised mission statements. Funding must be linked to results, not rhetoric.

Fourth, policy must stop overloading teachers with social missions. While well-being, equity, and engagement matter, they cannot substitute for instruction. Teachers are not therapists, and schools cannot fix every social ill. Narrowing their focus to teaching and learning is not a retreat from ambition—it is the path to achieving it.

Fifth, we need to take universities seriously again, not as businesses or ideological enclaves, but as communities of scholarship. That means free speech, rigorous standards, genuine admissions criteria, and less political micromanagement. It also means recognising that more degrees do not automatically mean a stronger economy or a fairer society. Quality and standards really matter.

None of these reforms requires massive new spending. What they require is clarity of purpose and political courage. The good news is that there are signs of movement. The national phonics check was one. So are recent discussions around behaviour standards and evidence-based instruction. Universities are starting to respond to an increasingly sceptical public. But these efforts are fragile and often contested. Without a coherent strategy—and the political will to see it through—they risk being swamped by the next wave of platitudes.

This book is not an argument against reform. It is an argument for smarter reform, rooted in evidence, driven by outcomes, and accountable to the public. If we want our students to succeed, our policies must stop dancing around failure and start demanding — and delivering — results.

Contributors

Rebecca Birch is Director of Research and Practice at a K-12 independent school in Sydney. She worked as a learning support officer in diverse settings while she undertook her teacher training after a successful career in advertising and fashion. Rebecca has provided consultation and content services for Ochre Education, Catholic Education Canberra Goulburn, and Catholic Education Tasmania. She has also appeared on panels for researchED and the Gonski Institute for Education. She holds a Bachelor of Arts from Macquarie University and a Bachelor of Teaching from the University of Technology, Sydney. Her current Master's research is on the links between explicit instruction, self-regulated learning and student wellbeing.

Robert Breunig, PhD, is Director of the Tax and Transfer Policy Institute at the Crawford School of Public Policy at the Australian National University and was previously Director of the Crawford School of Public Policy. He is one of Australia's leading Public Policy Economists and has published in over 75 international academic journals in economics and public policy. Professor Breunig has made significant policy impact through a number of his research projects: the relationship between childcare and women's labour supply; the effect of immigration to Australia on the labour market prospects of Australians; the effect of switching to cash from food stamps in the U.S. food stamp program and the inter-generational transmission of disadvantage.

Jennifer Buckingham, PhD, OAM is a former director of the Centre for Independent Studies education research program. While at the CIS, Jennifer published papers on reading, school choice, school funding, literacy, international assessments (including PISA), NAPLAN and My School, religious schools, boys' education, teacher training and employment, class size, and educational disadvantage. Jennifer has also written about childcare and female labour force participation. Jennifer's doctoral research was on literacy and social disadvantage. Jennifer has been at the forefront of debate on education matters for two decades, with hundreds of articles in major newspapers and regular radio and speaking appearances.

Deidre Clary is a former secondary English teacher and administrator in Australian schools. She has held academic appointments in Australia and USA where she specialized in teaching secondary English and literacy. More recently, at the University of South Carolina, she taught in the Master of Teaching program, and the online Master of Education program (ranked in top ten in the USA). In 2016-2018, Deidre joined the Australian Curriculum, Assessment and Reporting Authority (ACARA) where she led international curriculum comparison studies to inform the 2021 review of the Australian Curriculum. She is an occasional writer with the Centre of Independent Studies, *Quadrant* and the Page Research Centre.

Glenn Fahey is the Director of the Centre for Independent Studies Education program, with a particular focus on education finance and accountability. Before joining the CIS, Glenn held both policy- and research-intensive positions at the Centre for Educational Research and Innovation (OECD), Institute for Public Policy and Governance (University of Technology Sydney), and the Australian Treasury. Glenn's work has been published in academic journals including *Policy and Politics*, *Public Administration Quarterly*, and *Public Finance and Management,* as well as in the *OECD Education Working Paper Series*. He has been awarded a Master of Economics (University of New England), Master of International Relations (University of New South Wales), Bachelor of Economics (University of New South Wales), and Bachelor of Social Science (University of New South Wales).

David C Geary, PhD, is Curators' Professor and Thomas Jefferson Fellow in the Department of Psychological Sciences and Interdisciplinary Neuroscience Program at the University of Missouri in Columbia. He is a cognitive developmental and evolutionary psychologist with interests in mathematical cognition and learning. He is the author of several books spanning mathematical development and evolutionary foundations of individual differences, along with more than 300 articles and chapters across a wide range of topics. He has co-edited a five-volume book series, *Mathematical Cognition and Learning*. These volumes include *Evolutionary Origins and Early Development of Basic Number Processing*; *Development of Mathematical Cognition: Neural Substrates and Genetic Influences*; *Acquiring Complex Arithmetic Skills and Higher-Order Mathematical Concepts; Language and Culture In Mathematical Cognition*, and *Cognitive Foundations for Improving Mathematical Learning*.

Kerry Hempenstall, PhD, is a teacher and educational psychologist formerly in the Division of Psychology, RMIT University, where he had been an Associate Professor and manager of the Educational Psychology division of the RMIT Psychology Clinic. He is now in an honorary position as Senior Industry Fellow, School of Education, RMIT University. Prior to his commencement with RMIT in 1992, he had spent more than twenty years with the Victorian Education Department as a secondary teacher, social worker, and guidance officer (educational psychologist). Kerry was active in presenting workshops and papers at conferences, and he continues to publish in education journals (e.g., the Australian Journal of Learning Difficulties). He also participates in educational online forums, such as the DDOL Network for academics interested in literacy and effective teaching. He has also published numerous papers on educational topics.

Elizabeth M. Hughes, PhD, is Associate Professor of Special Education at The Pennsylvania State University. Her research evaluates literacy and mathematics interventions for students with disabilities and those considered to be at risk for the potential identification of a disability. She has published her research in several peer-reviewed journals, including *The Elementary School Journal, Teaching of Psychology, Journal of Autism and Developmental Disorders, and Teaching Exceptional Children*. She has developed interventions to support students' language when learning mathematics and answering open-response word problems in mathematics. She was previously an elementary teacher outside of Atlanta, Georgia, and interned with the Office of Special Education Programs (OSEP) through the U.S. Department of Education.

Trisha Jha is a Research Fellow in the Centre for Independent Studies Education program, where she leads a stream of work on the science of learning, as well as projects on school improvement and educational policy. Her recent publications include *What is the Science of Learning?, Implementing the Science of Learning: Teacher Experiences and Learning Lessons,* and *The future of Small-Group Tutoring.* She has also made submissions to and participated in a number of education inquiries. Trisha has previously had roles as a secondary teacher, including through the Teach for Australia program, in state and independent schools in regional Victoria. She has also worked as a senior policy adviser to opposition leaders in Victoria. She holds a Master's of Teaching with a specialisation in Research from Deakin University and a Bachelor of Arts in International Relations from the Australian National University.

Rob Joseph is a freelance data analyst specialising in education. He has provided analytical support across many projects and roles. He has previously held positions at CT Group, Transport for NSW, Ernst & Young and Catholic Schools NSW where he managed analytics across a sector comprising 596 schools and 263,000 students. Duties included benchmarking, board reporting, and preparing strategic analysis for schools and system authorities. Areas of analysis included enrolments, demographics, academic performance, financial performance, and workforce planning.

Tim McDonald, PhD is a former teacher and academic. He is the chief executive officer of the YMCA in Western Australia and a subject matter expert to the federal government's Engaged Classrooms Initiative, led by the Australian Education Research Organisation, which will develop practical resources for teachers on classroom management strategies, including routines and teacher skills. Dr McDonald was formerly the Executive Director of Catholic Education Western Australia and is the author of the 2010 book, Classroom Management: Engaging Students in Learning, now in its third edition.

Fiona Mueller PhD is an Adjunct Fellow at the Centre for Independent Studies and a former director of the CIS education research program. Her extensive practical experience led to her appointment as Head of

ANU College at the Australian National University and then Director of Curriculum at the Australian Curriculum, Assessment and Reporting Authority (ACARA) in Sydney. In 2019, the *Australian Financial Review's Power Issue* placed her among the top five most influential people in education. She is a Senior Fellow of Advance HE (formerly the Higher Education Academy) in York, UK. In April 2022, she was appointed to a three-year term on the Australian Curriculum, Assessment and Reporting Authority (ACARA) Board as the nominee of the Commonwealth Government

Kelly Norris is a Senior Research Associate at the Centre for Independent Studies, working on evidence-based identification and intervention processes for students with or at risk of maths difficulties. Prior to joining CIS in 2024, she has worked as a university lecturer, educational consultant, product developer, consultant teacher and classroom teacher with a particular focus on effective intervention within a multitiered system of support (MTSS). She holds a Bachelor of Education, Graduate Certificate of Education (learning difficulties) and Master of Education. In the latter research she investigated strategies and tools to improve identification and support for students with mathematical difficulties.

Andrew Norton, PhD is Professor of Higher Education Policy at the Monash Business School, Monash University. He is the author of *The Unchained University* (CIS, 2002), which sets out the case for a more market-driven higher education system. Andrew has also written widely on classical liberalism and on liberal and conservative political movements in Australia. Andrew worked at the CIS between the years of 1994 – 2011 with a break in the late 1990s, when he was Higher Education Adviser to Dr David Kemp, Federal Minister for Education, Training and Youth Affairs.

Corey Peltier, PhD is Assistant Professor of Special Education in the Department of Educational Psychology at the University of Oklahoma. His research interests include identifying effective interventions and assessment procedures to improve the mathematical outcomes for identified or at-risk for disabilities.

Sarah R. Powell is an Associate Professor in the Department of Special Education at The University of Texas at Austin and Associate Director of the Meadows Center for Preventing Educational Risk. Her research, teaching, and service focus on mathematics, particularly for students who experience mathematics differently. She is currently Principal Investigator (PI) of an Institute of Education Sciences (IES) efficacy grant (RAAMPS) related to word-problem solving at Grade 4, and is also PI of SPIRAL, an IES grant which works collaboratively with Grade 4 and 5 teachers who provide mathematics instruction to students with mathematics difficulty. She was awarded the Presidential Early Career Award for Scientists and Engineers in 2019.

Steven Schwartz, PhD AM, FASSA is a Senior Fellow at the Centre for Independent Studies. He writes mainly about education, freedom of speech and mental health. He is the author of more than a dozen books. Steven has served as Vice-Chancellor of Macquarie University in Sydney, Brunel University in London and Murdoch University in Perth. He also served as Chair of the Australian Curriculum, Assessment and Advisory Authority (ACARA). He was a Board member of Teach for Australia and is presently an Honorary Fellow at the University of Melbourne.

John Sweller PhD is an Adjunct Fellow at the Centre for Independent Studies. He is an educational psychologist and Emeritus Professor at the University of New South Wales. He is best known for formulating cognitive load theory, which uses our knowledge of evolutionary psychology and human cognitive architecture as a base for instructional design. The theory is one of the most highly cited educational psychology theories. It is a contributor to both research and debate on issues associated with human cognition, its links to evolution by natural selection, and the instructional consequences that follow. Based on hundreds of randomised, controlled studies carried out by many investigators from around the globe, the theory has generated a large range of novel instructional procedures. John has authored over 200 academic publications and is a Fellow of the Academy of Social Sciences in Australia.

Matthew Taylor was formerly Director of the Intergenerational program at the CIS which focuses on intergenerational inequality and the fiscal burden of government policy on future generations. Previously, Matthew held a research position at the Centre for Social Research and Methods at the Australian National University (ANU) and is currently a PhD candidate at the Crawford School of Public Policy at ANU. He was also previously at CIS from 2014 to 2015, working on paid parental leave and age pension policy. Matt has over a decade of experience in economic modelling and data analysis. Matt also formerly worked for a number of government agencies and universities including the National Centre for Social and Economic Modelling at the University of Canberra, the Commonwealth Department of Employment and the Australian Institute of Family Studies.

Joanna Williams is the founder and director of CIEO, an independent think tank in the United Kingdom. She is a weekly columnist for the online magazine *Spiked* and writes regularly for numerous other publications including *The Times, The Spectator, The Telegraph* and *The Daily Mail*. Joanna taught at the University of Kent for more than 10 years and was the director of Kent's Centre for the Study of Higher Education. Most recently, she worked as Head of Education and Culture at Policy Exchange. Her latest book, *How Woke Won* was published by Spiked in May 2022. She is also the author of *Women vs Feminism* (2017), A*cademic Freedom in an Age of Conformity* (2016) and *Consuming Higher Education: Why Learning Can't be Bought* (2011).

Acknowledgements

I wish to thank *The Australian, The Australian Financial Review, The Spectator Australia, EducationHQ, MultiLit, The Canberra Times, The Conversation, The Daily Telegraph,* and *The Sydney Morning Herald* for granting permission to reproduce previously published material in this volume. Their cooperation has enabled the inclusion of pieces that are essential to the arguments advanced in these pages. I am especially grateful to Karla Pincott, whose editing skills, research assistance, and wise counsel were fundamental to the creation of this book.

www.ingramcontent.com/pod-product-compliance
Lightning Source LLC
Chambersburg PA
CBHW070356240426
43671CB00013BA/2519